STEADFAST INK

American Embassy,
    Peiping, China, December 31st.

Dear Dr. Holzer:

On my return from Shanghai I found some very charming photographs which you were so thoughtful as to send me. I didn't realize that you had such talents along that line. I thought that the photograph of the coolies struggling with the heavy cart was particularly fine.

I note with pleasure that your wife's petition for preference quota status for yourself has been approved by the Department of Justice in record time. Congratulations are in order!

Sincerely yours,
Ringwalt

From Arthur Rumney Ringwalt, U.S. State Department Foreign Service Officer, Peiping, China (Peking/now Beijing), December 31, 1940

To Osvald "Valdik" Holzer, M.D.

Ringwalt references Valdik's new wife, Ruth (née Lequear) Holzer, regarding the embassy's quick work to secure a travel visa to America for Valdik to accompany her. The urgency of the moment followed the U.S. Embassy's advice to all foreigners in Peking to leave China as tensions were increasing between the U.S. and Japan.

What People Are Saying...

Steadfast Ink, the third in Schirm's book series about her Czech Jewish father, adds emotionally charged context to her research, adding a human face to history that echoes today. A must-read. As a Reference Archivist at the United States Holocaust Memorial Museum for over twenty years, I met Joanie Holzer Schirm in 2008. She had just begun her long journey to uncover the truths of what happened to forty-four paternal Jewish relatives who perished in the Holocaust. Sharing the same Czech heritage, we connected through our past and shared an interest in the remarkable voyage of discovery.

—Michlean Lowy Amir, former Reference Archivist, USHMM

Interweaving her recollections of her father's strong principles with her own journey of uncovering hidden truths of the past, in *Steadfast Ink*, Schirm brilliantly illustrates how intricate events and meaningful relationships shape our own lives and perceptions. As the world feels so disconnected, a look inward can uncover just how connected we all are.

—Nilam Patel, Center for International Studies Director/ELA Teacher
Orange County Public Schools, Orlando, Florida

Born and raised in Germany two generations after the darkest hours of German and human history, the recent events in American society disturbingly resemble those of a century ago. Today four generations removed from the Nazi terror on humanity, we American citizens are amid an attack by a minority on the heart and soul of our US Constitution and inalienable human rights, spewing conspiracies and alternative facts. In *Steadfast Ink*, Joanie Holzer Schirm as a gifted writer, brings her personal family story alive, putting a human face to facts and figures, reminding us that we must never remain silent.

—Christian J.G. Popp, Ph.D., CCO MINT Software Systems

Through a twist of fate, I learned of the first two books author Joanie Holzer Schirm had written about her father's life journey in fleeing from Hitler's wrath of World War II. I remember Dr. Holzer well. He was the Personnel Physician and did the entrance physical exams when my twin sister and I entered the Florida State Hospital School of Nursing in 1950, the locale of Joanie's first chapter in her new book, *Steadfast Ink*. Tears flowed as I read and felt this young man's sorrow as well as his courage. As with her first books, I am deeply grateful for her tireless efforts to tell more of her father's stories, ones we all need to hear, lest we forget.

—Lannie Varnes Boyd, Registered Nurse, Retired, Chattahoochee, FL

Joanie Holzer Schirm has a voice, and a heart needed now more than ever. I've known Joanie for over 25 years, watching, admiring, and learning from her as she poured her energies and considerable skills into leadership roles for many Orlando communitywide endeavors. Having read her first two books, *Steadfast Ink* once again reveals her passion for making a difference and her commitment to inspiring us all to become catalysts for positive changes to our fractious world.

—Marc Middleton, Founder/CEO, Growing Bolder, Host of Growing Bolder TV seen on public broadcasting stations nationwide

Having worked closely together with Joanie Holzer Schirm on her family story and uncovering all the layers of world history woven into it, I share the position it is more important than ever to share true stories from real individuals from the era of the Holocaust and its aftermath. As Holocaust survivors leave us now one after the other, we have to rely on the memories and artifacts they hand over to us as their heritage. We must share stories like those from *Steadfast Ink* to understand where antisemitism, hatred, and expulsion lead to, what it means to lose family roots and the trauma of rebuilding a new life somewhere else. The world demands such educational tools, now more than ever.

—Susanne Urban, Historian, former ITS (Arolsen Archives) Head of Historical Research

Steadfast Ink

The Journey Within

JOANIE HOLZER SCHIRM

Author of **Adventurers Against Their Will** and **My Dear Boy**

© 2021 by Joanie Schirm
All rights reserved by PeliPress imprint
Manufactured in the USA
ISBN 978-0-9886781-8-7 (hardcover)
ISBN 978-0-9886781-6-3 (paper)
ISBN 978-0-9886781-7-0 (e-Pub)
Unless otherwise noted, all images are used with permission of Joanie Schirm
Book design by Kate Winter
Library of Congress Cataloging-in-Publication (CIP) Data
Names: Schirm, Joanie Holzer, Author
First Edition September 2021
For Bulk Buying, contact: joanie@joanieschirm.com
www.joanieschirm.com

Contents

Introduction—The Ghost 1
Florida in Black and White 9
The Letter That Changed Everything 27
Steadfast Ink 43
How Schindler's List Led to Valdik's List 51
Looking to the East 59
What Was Known 69
My Czech Grandparents' Epitaph 75
Light Was Always There 107
The Reflection of the Viewer 131
What My Father Believed 139
Dealing With the Circumstance 151
Going Home 161
New Vines, Strong Roots 175
Epilogue: To Know the Place 191
Appendix
    Synchronicities From My Writing Journey 201
    More Than a Number - Holocaust in Bohemia and Moravia 225
    Biographies— Select Letter Writers and Family Members 227
Acknowledgments 235
About the Author 239

*To my Family. Then and Now.
Thank you for everything you taught me.*

*If we want a more just and peaceful world,
we must go in search of larger truths.
With that knowledge, we'll become
protagonists in shaping a humane future
that connects all living things.*

Introduction – The Ghost

> *"Hardship often prepares an ordinary person for an extraordinary destiny."*
>
> — C. S. LEWIS

Curiosity draws us to people and places vastly unlike ourselves. Ideally, we learn to understand and admire our differences rather than recoiling from one another. Most of us lead lives that have never been in jeopardy. Our lack of perilous experiences makes it all the more important to remember that this is not the case for many people in our world. Regime change, insurrections, war, persecution, famine, fire, or a hurricane can take away everything that matters—home, country, loved ones, possessions, identity—often in an instant. For those who survive, the next life chapter involves a struggle to adjust to a new way of being.

I am the daughter and granddaughter of survivors. For twelve years, I dug deep into my family's past, and in this book, I'll tell you what I found and how it felt.

To uncover my parents' meeting story, I didn't have to dig too deep. My two siblings and I knew that narrative well. Our parents-to-be met in the fall of 1940 in Peking (Beijing). Born in China of American missionaries, our Mom—Ruth Alice Lequear—at twenty-four, was a high-spirited schoolteacher traveling to a Christian mission school when she met a dashing twenty-nine-year-old Czech doctor—Oswald "Valdik" Holzer. A Jewish refugee, he'd found safe harbor in China after escaping the German Nazis a year earlier. From the first glance, it was romance. Six weeks later, they married. Their love affair lasted nearly sixty years until they died within two days of each other at the turn of the twenty-first century.

Valdik & Ruth, October 1940, Peking (Beijing)

I was a child in the 1950s growing up in sunny Florida when my father regaled me with his youthful adventures and forced displacement when the Nazis occupied his Czech Bohemian homeland as World War II simmered and boiled. I'd sit at Dad's side in our tropical riverside home while Dad spun remarkable tales. His descriptions of hair-raising escapes and escapades in exotic foreign lands held me spellbound. On occasion, I took copious notes, but mostly I listened and let my imagination run wild.

One day in my tenth grade English class, I heard my favorite teacher, Mrs. Bixby, describe what makes a great page-turner. "A *likable hero faces seemingly insurmountable odds and overcomes them, isn't sure who to trust on his journey through exotic locales with happenings that keep you on the edge of your seat.*" My dream of becoming an author took wings as I knew my father was feeding me the raw materials for a best seller. Still, life moved along—I grew consumed by school, marriage, children, career, and community activism. Five decades passed before I would uncover, as radio personality Paul Harvey used to say, "The rest of the story."

In February 2000, my siblings and I found a secret WWII letter collection my father had hidden in plain sight in antique Chinese red-lacquered boxes in our family home. Discovered after his death, some might describe the contents as Dad's ghost—the past that haunted him and lingered for the next generation to uncover. I chose those old letters as my inheritance and consider them the most incredible gift my Dad ever gave me: lasting pieces of him and much more. As I read the translated letters (written initially in my dad's native Czech by family members and friends), I learned they held power for us all. His story provides truths from a tumultuous migrant past detailing, like the physician my father was, a painful illness accompanied by a prescription for a better future.

When I read the letters, I realized when Dad had told me stories of his refugee years when I was a girl, he buffed away the sharp edges of immense personal pain. I devoured the massive correspondence—four hundred multi-paged missives from seventy-eight writers—and listened to Dad's long-forgotten details in seven hours of interviews I'd taped in 1989 and forgotten. The characters he met became as vivid and relevant to world history as those encountered by the fictional movie character Forrest Gump. They were people my Dad chanced upon before and during WWII that transformed the world with real consequences. They were seasoned by a time of tragedy and breathed, loved, hoped, failed, healed, or perished. All came to life in my mind's eye and heart.

Interview audiotapes from 1989

At first, I thought my job was to protect these mysterious missing correspondents' memory and dignity—mainly family and friends from Dad's bygone days. Then, as I mined the truth and made sense of it, I realized there was much more to my mission. A compelling narrative emerged, giving purpose to my relentless quest for understanding.

The people I learned about in the letters changed how I see my world. Their lives mattered. Their lessons are relevant regardless of who we are, where we came from, or what our ancestors went through as they searched for their safe harbor. When we dig into our family histories, we come to learn that a sense of the past helps us look toward the future and invites insight into our lives—our present. If you allow my Dad's words to enter your heart, you'll receive his compelling wish to teach, heal, and inspire a life of compassionate service, one that is formed by what you do with the messages you receive along the way.

My first two nonfiction books, *Adventurers Against Their Will* and *My Dear Boy*, go into great detail about my father's history, the letters, and much more. I hope you'll read them. *Adventurers Against Their Will* recounts my search for seven of dad's correspondents who became stateless and sought safety around the world during and after WWII. Seven decades later, I found two of these writers alive and descendants of all seven. I 'redelivered' their letters and recorded heart-wrenching tales they delivered in return. Their resilience of spirit taught me firsthand the importance of inspiring new generations not only to care but to *care enough* to protect human rights and dignity. I heard their stories of the

fragility of democratic systems that vanished while so many people stood by, expecting someone else to take action when they didn't.

My Dear Boy is my father's adventure and love story of how he roamed across five continents as a refugee and young doctor. One of his stops was China, where he was offered safe harbor in Shanghai and later in Peking (Beijing), and where in 1940 he met my mother. Like all young and in-love couples, they made dreams for their future together. I learned from the letters they had intended to stay in China and open a charity hospital and school. My mother was to run the school and my dad the hospital. Their dreams were deterred when Japanese warfare intensifying in the Pacific theater forced foreigners to evacuate.

After the war, my dad returned to China in 1946 with the United Nations Relief and Rehabilitation Administration, helping restore the devasted nation's healthcare system while also determining if Mom's and his dream hospital/school could be realized. The Chinese Communists drove the Americans out of the country. Democracy lost its chance to blossom and ended their dream.

Upon return to the United States, my father and mother began to explore whether they could go to Czechoslovakia, which had restored democracy after the Nazis were defeated. Perhaps my father could practice medicine there? The possibility ended in 1948 when the Communist Party took control of Czechoslovakia and properties were nationalized, homes seized, and democracy once again destroyed as it had been under the Nazis. I came to see how fragile democracies are and how freedom must be continuously nurtured and protected by the people, for the people.

On January 6, 2021, when the insurgent mob of President

Donald Trump supporters stormed the US Capitol in an attempt to stop the democratic process of America's Presidential election, I was grateful my parents weren't alive to witness the violent disdain for our democratic process. My father stayed in this country as a proud naturalized citizen because of the freedom provided by our democratic system. The treasonous insurrection and the failure of so many to condemn it would have destroyed him, reminding him of the losses he suffered and the inhumanity he left behind when he came to America.

Anton Chekhov wrote: *Love, friendship, respect do not unite people as much as a common hatred for something.* My father experienced what humans are capable of at their worst. Instead of succumbing to that darkness, Dad's goal turned to help others. And from his truths, I attempted to understand the matrix in which children learn to hate and adults believe it's okay to lie. History teaches, and we must listen.

As I wrote my first two books and examined past problems, I uncovered research, realizations, synchronicities, and anecdotes that didn't quite fit in either of my books but continued to inform my understanding. Primary, secondary, and tertiary sources provided more clues that needed to be shared. From my childhood admiration of the Nancy Drew book series, I now see her fictional sleuth character's formative influence on my life. Rather than accepting the cold facts of my dad's chaotic journey at face value, I live to find and share the human side of history and what it means for today and tomorrow.

Gathered here in *Steadfast Ink* is the stuff from my writerly "cutting room floor." I believe they add depth and richness to Dad's experience under the duress of conflict and the subsequent rebuilding of his life in America. These pages also provide information for people who, like me, traveled through genealogy and the narratives of their family's past to arrive at a deeper meaning in it all. Here, readers will learn more about my journey as I got to know my young dad and met his parents through their letters. I also share stories about my mother and the beauty and comfort she bestowed upon our family.

With perhaps the guidance from my mother's higher power, my destiny is to offer the letters and the truths I've uncovered to help mend hearts and change the way we live in our world. Beneath his tragedies and triumphs was a secret wish that inspired my father's compassionate life. If we all follow this desire, his blessing of a sort, the world will become a more caring and loving place. We must not settle for less.

I've done my best to stay as close to the facts as possible. My father was a grand storyteller, and thus, I've taken the opportunity to sustain his embellishments. My greatest hope is that Dad would be happy with the pieces I chose to pick up from my writer's floor and share with you. I hope these choices inspire you as they've continued to encourage me.

Thanks for staying on board. Onward. *Kupředu.*

Florida in Black and White

When I look back on my life, it feels like an endless summer in the best possible way, even though I don't recall the part that began in the north—North Florida, that is. That period between 1948 and mid-1952 was the end of a nomadic phase for my parents—Ruth Alice (née Lequear) and Oswald "Valdik" Holzer. Since they'd married in China in October 1940, they'd been searching and wondering where they belonged in the world. After leaving China in early 1941, they'd lived in Southern California, New York, Indiana, Peru, and Ecuador, and again in New York. When he applied to serve as a staff physician at the Florida State Hospital in Chattahoochee, Florida, my dad hoped the Sunshine State would ground and warm his soul.

After Dad's successful interview with the hospital in mid-1948, eager to get on with his new job, he returned to New York and packed his pregnant wife and my soon-to-be elder siblings—Tommy and Patty—into our black Ford sedan. I made my first trip to the Florida Panhandle in the summer of 1948, five months before I was born, sheltered in the darkness of my mother's womb. American motoring was still a few years shy of Interstate highways and air conditioning, so my parents wound their way through a maze of two-lane roads as the searing heat and dust of a Deep South July rushed into the open car windows.

The Panhandle is the stretch of North Florida that arcs west for about a hundred miles along the Gulf of Mexico from the white sand beaches at its southern fringe north to the Georgia and Alabama borders. The region resembles a handle on a map you could use to pick up the entire state to turn it upside down and pour out the soupy residue of tropical rain.

In December, I was born in the small town of Chattahoochee, about two hundred miles due east of Mobile, Alabama, and a peach pit toss south of the Georgia border. If you picture Florida as Miami Beach or even Disney World, you're thinking of a very different place. You're less likely to find swaying palms in North Florida than tall, rough-barked cypress and live oaks with long, lazy limbs draped in hanging moss. We seldom saw tourists from New Jersey in Bermuda shorts, and Speedos were rare. In Chattahoochee, this remains the case even today.

When I officially emerged through a fog of amniotic fluid into the light of the world, a giant full moon and a heavenly configuration, described by astrologers as a Sagittarius Sun and Sagittarius rising, provided a fanfare. With this double Sagittarius alignment, my future disposition was expected to be generally optimistic, lighthearted, and intent on enjoyment and adventure. Beyond the implications of planetary alignment affecting my personality, I also subscribe to the truth Arnošt, my paternal Czech grandfather, gave my father on what impacts one's persona: "We are born to the land as well as to our mother."

Chattahoochee, which got its name from the Creek Indian word meaning "pounded rock," sits high on a bluff overlooking the bass-rich Apalachicola River—or, as locals called it, the *RIV*-uh. In 1948, Floridians had a more colorful name for Florida State Hospital, originally the Florida Asylum, where Dad was to work—they called it "The Crazy House." The hospital had been the state's repository for the mentally ill since 1876, a part of Florida lore, as infamous as it was famous. Notable patients included an ax murderer whose slaying of his family in 1933 influenced the notion that marijuana led to criminal insanity. The month I was born there, records show I was the only person "admitted by birth" versus "committed."

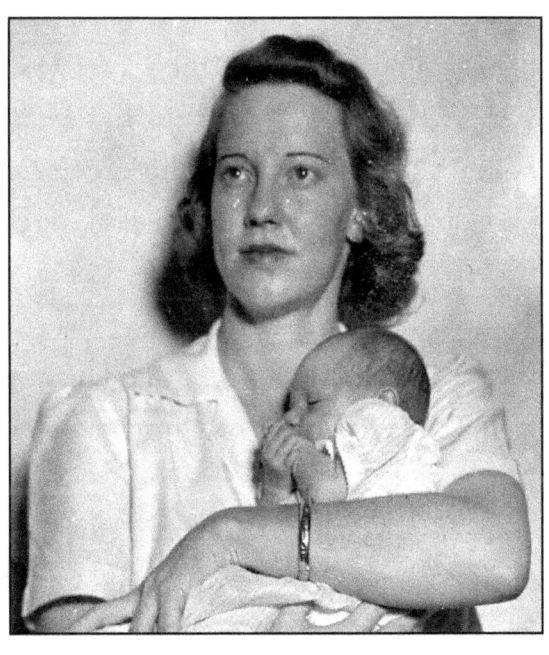

Ruth and daughter Joanie, December 1948

Chattahoochee was as foreign as almost anywhere Dad might have picked on the globe to serve as a Czech doctor. The inhabitants' languid drawl was as thick as their prized Tupelo honey and as unshakeable as their devotion to the Southern way of life. Like many places in the Deep South, the hospital divided the white people from Black and called them "coloreds."

From the start, my dad took offense when his receptionist Lillian prioritized whites over the Black people, regardless of who arrived first in the waiting room. He told her the patients needed to be treated equally and to amend her system. She responded: "The white ones always go first. The coloreds have to wait their turn." He told her that would change, to which she replied, "Well, in that case, I quit." Lillian marched over to Dad's new boss and complained about the foreign guy. The administrator left my father no option but to return to "the way it was." The director's comments were explicit: "Are you trying to start a race riot? Don't be foolish. Follow the rules." Dad got his orders, and the next day Lillian was back on the job. She continued calling the white patients first while Dad steamed in the unrelenting humidity.

Southern segregation must have struck my father as chillingly similar to what happened to his family and friends in Prague. Instead of the separation of Jews from non-Jews with signs of "No Jews Allowed" or "No Jews or Dogs allowed," signs on bathrooms and other facilities at Florida State Hospital and throughout the town read: "Whites Only" or "Colored Only." Rules regarding housing, schools, and lunch counters were rigidly enforced. The human rights violations didn't stop with segregation. During my dad's first weeks in Chattahoochee, he learned that eight Black people had been lynched over the past fifty years in nearby Jackson County, most recently in the courthouse square of Marianna, Florida, just fourteen years before. In 2015, I learned from the Equal Justice Initiative report about "racial terror lynchings" across the American South. The total number of African American victims of lynching by white Floridians from 1877-1950 was three hundred and thirty-one. That was just the number that EJI knew of from their early research. Likely now more. Nine of these were in Jackson County. Chattahoochee's Gadsden County lynched four more innocent souls.

Until they arrived, I suspect our new family to the area had little knowledge of the atrocities that came before them. If my father had, perhaps he'd have chosen another job elsewhere. Soon they'd understand the South's treatment of those they saw as inferior humans, much like the Nazis categorized my father's side of the family.

Our family moved into one of the typical pinewood-frame vernacular houses surrounding the hospital made available to white staff upon arrival. Florida pine is harder than most lumber, producing excellent weather-resistant building material. It also attained a place inside our home, thanks to my father's many skills. Soon after moving in, Dad built a desk using wood from a torn-down house. He created his masterpiece featuring handles and hinges of genuine Chinese brass brought to America by my parents in 1941. My father formed the desk in two pieces, painting the top and sides in a shiny black lacquer and lightly staining the remaining pinewood a dark, handsome brown.

Valdik, Patty, Joanie, Tommy, 1949

Chinese desk

For the next sixty years, that desk followed our family from house to house. It served as a storage area for childhood board games, playing cards, and assorted papers, including the letter that changed everything in my father's life, addressed to *My Dear Boy*, which you'll learn more about in the next chapter.

After Chattahoochee, the desk's next destination was Chipley, Florida. I was little more than a toddler in May 1951 when my father left his position as personnel physician and chief of the orthopedic services at the State mental hospital and joined the staff of a new public hospital in Chipley, forty-five miles west of Chattahoochee. Unless you're from the Florida Panhandle, you've probably never heard of Chipley and couldn't find it on a map without the help of a magnifying glass or Google Earth. Yet somehow, the Communists who'd taken over my father's homeland in 1948 located him there.

In early 1952, Dad opened his mail to find an invoice from the Communist regime in Czechoslovakia for back taxes on Benešov property that his grandmother had owned. In 1942, the Nazis confiscated his family's combined birthplace, family home, and family-run grocery store. After WWII, it was returned to relatives for 'safekeeping' as they assumed dad would retrieve it. Ten years later, the story involved the communists' intended heist. Dad marched down to the Western Union office and, in his thick Czech accent with nasalized vowels, asked to send a telegram that read: *Polib mi prdel!*

With no knowledge of what she was transmitting, the innocent clerk forwarded to the Communist government in Czechoslovakia the official message: "Kiss my ass!" This defiant tale became one of my favorite childhood stories.

Later that year, opportunity lured my parents to Brevard County, a small but fast-growing area of Florida in need of doctors. Shortly after their arrival, they bought a small, coquina shell house on a skinny barrier island. The Atlantic Ocean to the east

Joanie, Patty, Tommy, 1954

and the Indian River to the west, separating the island from the mainland. Islands stand only by the whim of fate, a foothold surrounded by chaos. It seemed a fitting terrain for my Dad following the previous decade of his life. The changeability of an island offered my parents a new beginning, offering a hopeful chance for renewal.

Across the bridge on the mainland, my father established his general medical practice in downtown Melbourne, an east coast town of 3,500 about halfway between Miami and Jacksonville. At the time, there were only six doctors on Brevard Hospital's[1] staff. While living in Chattahoochee, my father was a full member of the Florida State Medical Association. Still, in Brevard County, he was forced to be an "on-trial" associate for one year. Because Dad was the first foreign-born doctor the hospital had ever encountered, the staff and the twenty-one-member Brevard County Medical Society did not entirely welcome him.

Their cold shoulder may have been due to the national political atmosphere. In 1950, Wisconsin Senator Joseph McCarthy began carrying out his infamous witch hunts for communists in America. Anyone who had a thick European accent was suspected of being part of the "Red Menace." My father was not a candidate for believing in communism on any level, especially since communists had recently taken over his homeland. Florida was overrun with suspicious attitudes, with some cities like Jacksonville enacting anti-communist ordinances, banning "any Communist from being

---

[1] Now Holmes Regional Medical Center

within the city limits."²

It was also a time in America when immigrants were expected to assimilate, not the other way around. That may explain why my father never taught his children the Czech language, one of my great regrets. He felt we'd be safer mixed into the American melting pot.

Shortly after we arrived on the island, another person was stirred into our family melting pot when Iola Williams, 54, joined us. Iola was an African American patient of my dad's from Chipley, suffering from phlebitis. Her painful inflammation made the veins in her legs swell. Iola believed she was in danger of death from a blood clot if my father wasn't nearby to treat her condition. When Iola's husband passed away

Iola Williams with Patty & Joanie, 1956

and her children were on their own, she asked to join us as housekeeper and nanny. My parents set up a bedroom for Iola, and for the next ten years, she served as my second mother, as beloved as the first. While my sister, Patty, and brother, Tommy, nicknamed

---

² Wikipedia: *McCarthyism: Freedom Under Fire* by Michael Linfield, 1990 South End Press

me "Nuisance" as I sometimes unleashed my inner charm monster, Iola chose to call me "Sugar," which came out to me as "Su-gah." Not only did she help me learn to control my inner charm monster, Iola also soothed my little soul. It didn't hurt that Iola made the best fried chicken I've ever tasted. One day, as I sat on her broad lap, admiring the ebony color on the top of her hands swirling into contrast to her pink palms, she told me in a whisper that my dad was the only doctor who'd ever treated her with respect. At the time, I was too little to understand fully what that meant. I do now and do not doubt that Iola was sharing the truth.

Soon after Iola arrived, my mom's parents—Horace and Emma Lequear, or Padi and Nani as we called them—moved to Florida. Their history had begun in China, three decades before my parents serendipitously found each other there. My grandfather arrived in Hunan Province in 1906 as a missionary on his way to the Christian mission field in Huping (Lakeside) College, Yochow. Padi was from Doylestown, Pennsylvania, and went to China as a teacher under the Reformed Church foreign mission board. My grandmother Nani, born Emma Martha Kroeger of

Nani and Padi, 1949

Akron, Ohio, went to China under the auspices of the same foreign mission board and arrived in 1911 as a supervising nurse. Their friendship began during her first night at the mission's dining table and slowly bloomed until they married in 1913. Their first daughter Ruth Alice, my mom, was born in Huping in 1916. Among the Lequear family acquaintances was the novelist and missionary Pearl S. Buck. In 1926, amid a tremendous anti-foreigner, anti-Christian upheaval, Padi and Nani and their four children returned to America on their third furlough. They were among many who never returned to the Chinese mission fields.

After holding pastorates as a Christian minister in Pennsylvania and Virginia, my grandfather had a slight stroke. My parents built a small house for Padi and Nani adjacent to ours. In 1957, we left the spectacular sunrises over the Atlantic Ocean, moving into a larger, multilevel dream home built on Fisherman's Point on the other side of the narrow barrier island, along the Indian River shore. Although not a river at all—more precisely an estuary and a lagoon—there, nearly every evening, we witnessed a spectrum of beautiful red- and orange-tinted sunsets over brackish waters filled with dolphins, manatees, birds, and other wildlife.

Dad's private medical practice in downtown Melbourne was slow to develop until the wife of a vice president of Northrop Corporation brought her daughter for treatment. Northrop was one of the three contractors at Patrick Air Force Base and Cape Canaveral, where the government was inaugurating the Space Age by testing pilotless jet planes flying at a speed of sound. Cape Canaveral was the key to a vast over-water flight area devoid of shipping lanes or populated land masses. As my dad described it, the jets would race halfway across the Atlantic and then drop in the water when fuel ran out. This emerging Long-Range Proving Ground later became Kennedy Space Center.

The Northrop executive's wife liked my father immediately. She was charmed by his lingering accent and continental demeanor, deemed him brilliant "for a small town," and spread the word. Before long, Dad was the physician for all three experimental space-engineering companies, conducting their pre-employment examinations and taking care of their workers' compensation cases. He performed an increasing number of pre-employment exams for missile contractor employees—from around 700 his first year to 1,600 just five years later. All the while, he was developing his family medical practice, establishing him as a beloved "Doc" in the community for the next thirty-four years.

The nearby sandbar along the edge of Indian River Lagoon, where my friends and I often played, taught me a valuable lesson. The surrounding tidal ebb and flow, tinged with a saltwater scent, formed my view of the world. It showed me that life is more complicated than what appears on the surface. Sometimes things can seem in place until a rogue wave or changing tides washes them away. This childhood encounter helped me understand the concept of renewal and second chances.

One of my earliest memories of my father involves me at age ten, next to him on a sofa in our new home with twelve-foot windows overlooking the river. Following an afternoon of playing tag in the

Car bonding – Valdik & Joanie

swimming pool, we watched the glow of our black-and-white television while Dad's healing hands rubbed my small, tired back, and we snuggled as children and their parents often do.

    From such special moments grew my joy and a father-daughter bond, which was often tested but never broken as I became involved in my network of fun-seeking, sunburned friends during the rebellious rock-and-roll 1960s. As a young teen, I was carefree and mischievous. Always up for sneaking out of the house for a nocturnal swim in the phosphorescent iridescent green of the ocean, as the glowing jostled waters appeared like tiny twinkling stars suspended in the salt water. Or perhaps for a night canoe cruise on the river in the moonlight. The best adventures started with running away from home; always with a companion, every escapade involved a little risk.

My youth's memories are full of the Beach Boys' Surfin' Safari songs. The summers of 1963 and 1964 meant nonstop water-skiing on the river, interrupted only by long, leisurely lunches with my girlfriends Amy, Ann, Stephanie, Nina, Jerrie, and Kathe. In the bright sun, we sat in our skimpy bathing suits by the Eau Gallie Yacht Club pool, where our food and drink appeared free, as we signed our names to the bills using our parents' club membership numbers. It was heaven . . . until "the incident" happened, and my plans for the summer of 1965, just before my senior year at Melbourne High School, took an unexpected turn.

For as long as I can recall, my dad had the coolest cars in town. At one point, a blue convertible, six-cylinder Alfa Romeo Giulia Spider, with vanity license plates reading "Bohemia 1," was parked in our garage. Then Porsche designers brought the 911 into the world. My parents were traveling in Europe in 1963 when they saw the rare model of automobiles at the International Motor Show in Frankfurt. Soon after, my dad placed his order for a beautiful white, two-door coupé. Technically a four-seater, it wasn't much of a family car with the tiny rear seats. The 911 "Porsh-a" was my father's tooling-around machine, and upon delivery, had the whole town talking.

Porsche automobiles are objects of fascination for all kinds of people, of whom I am one. Late in dad's life, when he reminisced about his 911, I remember him saying that Porsche DNA includes courage, creativity, and a fighting spirit. "Much like you," he added with a grin. Still young enough to tool around at age seventy-two, I finally acquired one and was welcomed into the Porsche family. Just like my dad, their appearance and sense of fun and freedom speak to me.

When I was sixteen, while my parents were absent from the house one dark, steamy evening, I "borrowed" my father's Porsche 911. With its awe-inspiring six-cylinder revving capacity, I headed out for a joyride with my equally fun-loving friend Stephanie Sawyer.

My misadventure coincided with the impending completion of US Interstate 95, slightly west of where we lived, across the island bridge onto the mainland.

Valdik & Ruth, Indialantic, circa 1960s

A long, freshly paved straightaway lay before us. You could still smell the tar. Of course, the highway was barricaded and legally off-limits. Still, word had gotten out among the teenage population that this was the perfect place for a fast drive without adult interference. It was to be a night of pure exhilaration on the open road.

I won't describe the whole escapade, but Steph and I reached a speedometer reading of well over 100 miles per hour. We did this with the windows open, warm, humid air whipping through my long strawberry-blond locks, and Steph's sun-kissed long brown hair. Squealing with joy, adrenalin rushing through my veins, I shifted gears. The Beach Boys were blasting from the speakers when the putrid smell of burning rubber engulfed us. As I pulled the car over and began looking around, I noticed the emergency brake was still on. And then, the engine wouldn't start back up. After that, my memory is somewhat foggy.

I do remember standing next to the Porsche bawling like a two-year-old whose bottom was stinging the kind of brush-handle spanking that was acceptable in those times. Steph's stunned expression is embossed on my memory. For what seemed like forever, we walked in the mosquito-laced West Melbourne darkness to a store's payphone to call for help. At least my father wasn't around to see his much-loved Porsche dangling from the hook behind a tow truck as it inched past the towering royal palm trees that lined our long driveway.

The incident didn't remain a private affair beyond that first night as word spread everywhere. The tow-truck driver happened to be one of my father's patients, and he felt obligated to relay all the gory details. Despite this, my father did not spew smoke or steam as his disabled car had.

"Luckily, making cars that are fast yet still easy to control is a chief design objective of Ferdinand Porsche," he said as he sat me down. "Some things that you try in life test your judgment. You failed."

A Porsche 911 emergency brake was very expensive, so my punishment was to spend my entire summer vacation working as a receptionist at my father's medical practice instead of surfing and water-skiing with my friends. Delivering his disciplinary action with a sinister grin, Dad pointed out that his office, overlooking the Indian River, would give me a magnificent view of other water skiers throughout the day.

Despite how I came to it, I grew to like the job, coworkers, and the patients, who ranged from professionals involved with the burgeoning space program to indigents who lacked financial resources to pay their bills. The latter were mainly fishing families from tiny towns to the south like Grant and Micco. African American families walked to my father's office from the neighborhood two miles across the railroad tracks known in those days as "Colored Town." Dad saw every patient in the order in which they arrived.

During that summer, I developed a great admiration for my father's strict instruction to treat all patients equally, no matter their financial circumstances. For those he knew could not afford the care, my dad always marked bills with the letters "NC," meaning "no charge." Whenever an NC patient came to the window, my instructions were to smile and say, "Thank you for coming to see Dr. Holzer. Today there is no charge for his services."

One evening, as the summer of 1965 was drawing to a close, my father and I set out for our drive home across the two-mile causeway spanning the glorious Indian River. As the sunset painted bright orange ribbons across the water, I told him I was impressed by his generosity, but it seemed to me he saw an awful lot of people for free. Why did he do it?

Dad was quiet for a long time. The radio was off, and the only sound was the hum of Porsche's powerful engine. The car then slowed a little. He gripped the black leather covering his steering wheel a bit more tightly, looked at me for a moment with his sad gray eyes, and in a barely audible voice replied, "I'm trying to help the suffering humanity the best way I know how."

That was all he said. I didn't know then that my destiny was to uncover the inspiration for those words.

The Letter That Changed Everything

With several translators working on the four hundred letters that my father preserved after WWII, the English versions of the forty-four from my grandparents arrived slowly from April 2008 to August 2009 and in random date sequence. *My Dear Boy* readers encounter my grandparents in a chronological and gradual way, but my relationship with them started in a much more dramatic one: instant affection.

It was a love affair I might not have known if I hadn't made a final, fortuitous choice as my brother, sister, and I pored through our parents' possessions. Perhaps as a part of my early Presbyterian upbringing, I believe that some things may be predestined. I will never accept it as merely a matter of chance that one of the last mementos I chose for my inheritance was the Chinese-style desk my father built in Chattahoochee the year I was born.

Like the lacquered boxes where I found the letters, the desk had been a presence in my life as it traveled with us from home to home. And again, like the boxes—its contents were unknown to my siblings and me until we began our sorting and sifting after our elderly parents died. When I first hastily opened the desk's bottom cabinet, I noticed some files and papers tucked behind long-neglected board games, but I didn't stop to examine them. There was too much to do, too many other papers to read. In the chaos of culling through everything my father left behind, I relegated the matter of examining the desk to a date in the future. After choosing the desk as part of my inheritance in 2000, it came home with me. For eight years, it remained there, primarily untouched except when I dug out the games for my grandchildren.

I can tell you the exact date when I finally opened the desk cabinet again. It was April 2, 2008. In the years after my parents died, I had visited my letter trove from time to time but only briefly. I would remove the letters from the storage closet and examine just a few, as a paleontologist might select a single bone from a skeleton. The sheer volume was overwhelming. The experience was as if I had reached a seashore and found not one message in a bottle but hundreds.

Each time I read one of the few letters written in English, I slipped from present-day sunny Florida into the dark world of World War II and the Holocaust. Regarding lives lost and cities destroyed, this was the most devastating conflict in human history, and now I was immersed in it. The emotions were too difficult to handle at that time in my life. I was running my busy engineering company, my daughter Kelly was away at college, my son Derick was very young, and my second husband, Roger Neiswender, needed my attention, too. I had little occasion to contemplate my dad's connections to the letter writers and what had happened in his youth. After a few minutes, I would slip the letters back into their plastic storage bins, stack them in the closet, and close the door.

In January 2008, eight years after my parents' deaths, I sold my company after thirty-five years in the engineering business. The transition from business owner to the full-time explorer of family history excited me. I had important work to do. I began my retirement by slipping the old multi-page letters into protective plastic covers and assigning a number to each as I prepared to scan them electronically. I noticed many letters from people whose names were unfamiliar. I assumed some were college friends from Dad's days at Charles University; others were likely people he had met in China or Czechs who, like him, had emigrated to escape the Nazi terror. Whenever I recognized the name of a murdered relative, a deep sadness overtook me.

I was almost finished with the mammoth project when something told me to revisit the desk. There was no longer any reason to wait. I opened the bottom cabinet and carefully removed the documents. I found my father's 1922 graduation notice from the equivalent of an American middle school. There was documentation of his United Nations Relief and Rehabilitation Administration (UNRRA) service in China soon after World War II. As a physician, he helped that nation recover from the crippling effects of eight years of war. Later, I would learn that UNRRA, primarily dominated by the United States, represented forty-four nations after WWII, coordinating distribution of food, fuel, clothing, shelter, and other necessities, medical and other essential services. My father was assigned to China relief efforts as a physician. While there in 1946 and 1947, he reorganized the surgical service at Peiping Municipal Hospital, was an instructor at Pei Ta (Peking University, regarded by some as "China's Harvard"), and served as a consulting surgeon for the National Health Administration.

Within the desk, I found several Czech letters dated 1945-48 from Benešov relatives. I recognized names and places and realized their significance must be enormous. I pondered if these letters might be the ones that revealed the fates of my father's family and friends. "If only I had learned to read and speak Czech," I muttered.

Safely stored in the bottom back corner of the desk cabinet, I found five handwritten letters sent from my father in China to my mother in Virginia between 1946 and 1947. After spending the first two months of my retirement sorting through letters written between 1939 and 1944, it was nice to see some dated after the war and written in English. My mom lived with her parents, tending to my two older siblings. She missed Dad tremendously during that year spent apart. It filled me with joy to read how Dad addressed my mother by her childhood nickname: "My *dearest Chick,*" "*Darling Chickie,*" "*Dearest Chick and kids, and Darlings.*" Most signed with a familiar "Love and Kisses" and "Bub" or "Bubbie," the nickname given to my dad during the second half of his life.

As I sat on the floor by the desk, reading the letters, their tone was instantly familiar—colorful descriptions of Dad's exciting life and of the places my parents had traveled together in China. The letters gave no hint that Dad was troubled about his parents' horrendous deaths. I worried about his emotional state. Instead of letting his grief out, he seemed to be keeping it bottled up, deep inside, where it could cause the most damage. As I read the letters written in English in chronological order, it was evident he continued with his life as if nothing had happened and had put up a protective wall to conceal his true feelings. He didn't mourn, at least publicly. He presented a warm and cheerful facade, never revealing his incomplete grief or what he held in his unhealed memory.

I began to imagine my father on the verge of becoming emotionally irretrievable. His wound was not something you just sewed up with stitches and forgot. Since he willingly left Mom behind for a year in America, I harbored a deep fear about the state of their marriage. But just like so many of my other revelations, these letters "arrived" at the moment I needed them most. I got to see dad's messages of affection and appreciation for my mother expressed playfully. His lifeline was intact, and his hope of togetherness had come true. Like drinking a glass of warm milk before bed, the letters gave me peace.

Joanie discovering Arnost's last letter written to son Valdik, April 2008

For his birthday greeting letter on February 7, 1947, he wrote:

> Darling Chickie,
> This letter is just for you for your birthday ... it is a happy day for me too because I received your letter from January 14. I hope

that this is the only birthday we will ever be separated and the next one we will be with the whole family in our own little home—Hao pu Hao? (Is that all right?)

I love you and miss you like H—. I love you twice as much because you love the babies . . . Well, this is the end again, and I hope that there will be another letter in the mail soon.

Love and Kisses, Bub.

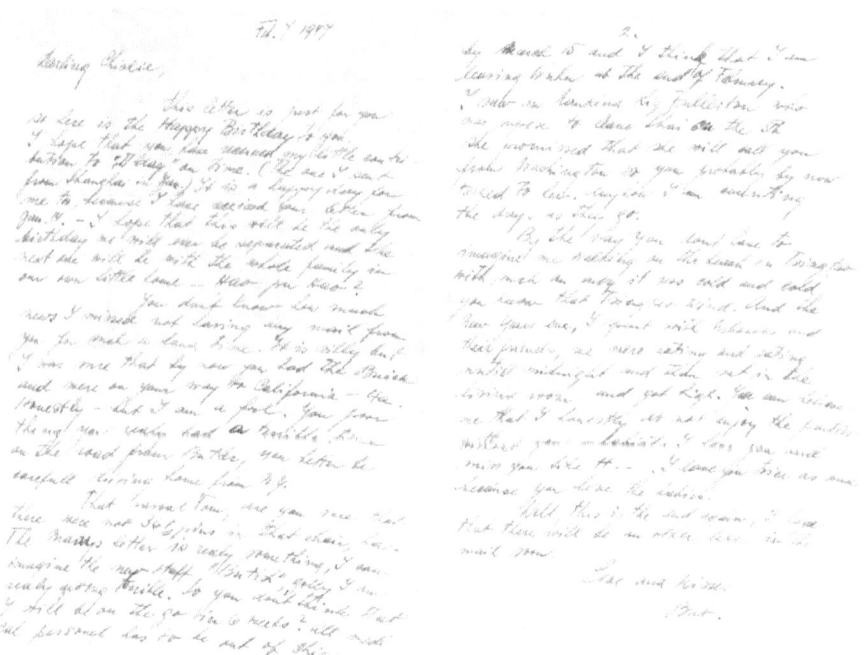

Valdik to Ruth, while working for UNRRA 1947

It was probably the only birthday they were apart in almost sixty years of marriage.

My favorite line is when he told her he expected to be home soon:

Declared as surplus next week, and I can't wait any longer . . . I have ants in my pants.

His words put me back on top of the world—and then, I retrieved another letter that sent me plummeting off its farthest edge. Hidden between two official 1946 documents related to Dad's relief efforts for the United Nations was a small, tan envelope with three Czech words handwritten in blue ink: *Můj drahý Valdíku* (My dear Valdik). Gently, I looked into the envelope, which someone had sliced open at the top with a letter opener. Inside, yellowed with age, was a single small folded page.

I did not immediately recognize my grandfather's handwriting as he typed most of his letters. But as I stared at the back of the page, my eyes drifted down to the signature in Czech: *Táta* or Dad. Arnošt's cursive handwriting was beautiful. I turned the letter over to look at the date on the front: *21. Duben 1942*.

'Duben' meant April. By then, I knew the Nazi transport documentation for my grandparents from Prague to Terezín was dated April 24, 1942—written three days before they were sent to the concentration camp. My hands began to tremble as I realized what I was holding. Likely, the last letter from my grandfather to my father. What did it say?

All the other envelopes had gone through official government mail service and bore traces of Nazi inspection: *Geöffnet*, meaning *opened by*; or a stamped swastika. This envelope bore no markings and wasn't censored by the Germans. It must have somehow been delivered to my father directly. My grandfather had been able to speak his mind freely. At this moment, the curtain rose. My life that lay ahead as an investigator, chronicler, and disseminator of the letters was revealed.

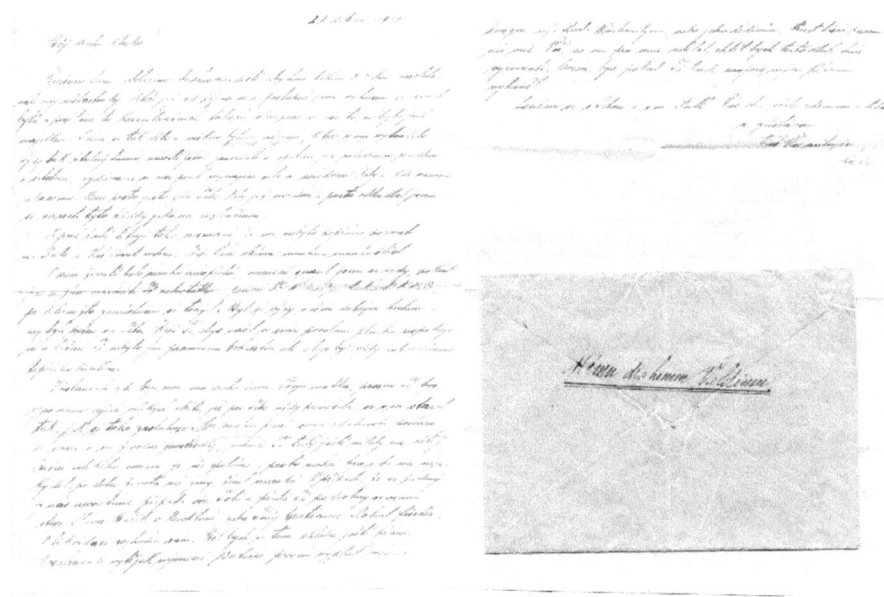

Last letter, written in the Czech language from Arnost to son Valdik

I made arrangements to have all the letters written in Czech translated right away. Just two weeks before, I'd tried to locate a translator through a local Winter Park museum that honored the famous Czech artist Albín Polášek. The director recommended a woman named Petra Míšková, who had done translation for the museum.

Petra cheerfully agreed to help. She worked on the "My dear Valdik" letter right away but had difficulty as the cursive writing was in "Czech old style," used in her homeland before she was born. What Petra could decipher was very, very sad. She saw the name "Ruth" and other family names and said it would take her several days to decipher. I was dismayed by the delay and shared my frustration with my friend Charley Williams. He reminded me that his girlfriend's sister was married to Mirek Katzl, a multi-talented Czech who had translated five books into English. At Charley's urging, Arnošt's letter took flight once again via modern email as I forwarded the scan to Mirek.

There is an art to translation. Correct word choice is essential to preserving the original author's intent. A poorly chosen word may start a narrative on a new and sometimes misguided course. There is no such thing as a literal translation, and thus I began to understand Mirek needed to take his time to produce his translation of Arnošt's words.

One day after finding the letter, I celebrated my retirement from Geotechnical and Environmental Consultants (GEC), the Orlando firm I'd co-founded and served as president for seventeen years. The party was a happy springtime gathering of colleagues, family, friends, and the carefree island songs of my favorite ocean-loving musician, Jimmy Buffett. A combined celebration of the life I had just left and the new journey I was embarking on. It was also the day that Mirek translated the letter. But in a meant-to-be twist of fate, the translation did not reach me until the following day.

When Mirek's wife, Valli, phoned with a heads-up that his email was coming, she suggested I not be alone when I read it. In town for the party, my son Derick, then twenty-three, had serendipitously stayed on for one more day. He was eager to sit at my side as I read the letter. Providence was at work. This first translation I received from the treasure trove of letters was likely my grandfather's final letter and provided me the first opportunity to meet him.

Taking a deep breath, as a time traveler, I stepped back to April 21, 1942, and began reading Arnošt's letter aloud to my son:

My dear boy,

Today we are leaving for an assembly point so that in three or four days, we can follow the fate of those unfortunate people who have been, since last October, gradually chased out of their homes and sent to concentration camps, robbed of everything they had. This happened to us as well, and we had to leave the ground floor and its furnishings, the flat that had always been such a cozy home to us.

Arnošt Holzer

Carrying only the necessary clothes, we are setting out on a journey, not knowing the day of our return or when and where we might be united again. I am not certain whether I will get to see you ever again, so I decided to write these lines as my goodbye to you.

I deeply regret that I wasn't able to know Ruth and your family life. I wish both of you much, much happiness.

I had a lot of failures in my life. However, when possible, I have tried to spare you from my shortcomings and help you become a doctor, a profession you always sought. You have always been a good boy, and we are proud of you. I wish for you to find full satisfaction in your profession. I also wish that your profession of curing doesn't just become a source of wealth for you, but that you yourself become a benefactor to the suffering humanity.

By the time I reached my grandfather's wish for my father's life, I was sobbing beyond control. My son, with his arm gently placed on my shoulders, said, "Mom, I'll read the rest." Derick continued Arnošt's words:

> Should my dear wife, your mother, be left without me, I implore you to remember the great sacrifices she always made for you and to take care of her the way she deserves. She has a small pension that she herself earned and secured, thus her means of living. She will never be a burden to you. I myself don't have much property; everything is communal with your mother. Therefore, I don't want you to ask for your property share from my wife during her life.
>
> In case we don't see each other, everything will go to you. Your Uncle Sláva Mařík of Neveklov or cousin Robert Fischer should give you a detailed list of the property. You then decide how to liquidate the inheritance. I have one more wish in that respect. If, after all the expenses, you are left with at least 30 thousand Czech crowns, please pay my brother-in-law, Rudolf Winternitz, or his descendants, the sum of thirty thousand. For everything he has done for me, I would like to pay my debt to him in this moment. If you can, please fulfill my wishes.
>
> With warm kisses and greetings, I bid you both, you and Ruth a farewell. I remain,
>
> Your loving táta

At first, Derick had read calmly. Then he too began to weep. Arm in arm, my son and I sat together crying, soaking the couch, for what seemed like a very long time. Without a doubt, it was the saddest letter I've ever read. I felt such deep appreciation for Mirek for his introduction to the grandfather I could never meet. To my very core, I understood the significance of my father's benevolent life—caring for those most in need.

> I wish for you to find full satisfaction in your profession. I also wish

that your profession of curing doesn't just become a source of wealth for you, but that you yourself become a benefactor to the suffering humanity.

Months later, through another translated letter, I learned that before Arnošt and Olga were on their way to the Nazi train transport, he gave the letter to his sister, Valda Mařík. The latter escaped deportation partially because her husband wasn't Jewish. She safeguarded Arnošt's message until she could finally mail it to my dad after the war. I could picture my father holding this letter in his hands on the porch in Ecuador, where my parents lived in 1945 before moving back to the United States.

Arnošt and Olga, 1941

I tried to guess what thoughts flooded my Dad's mind. Czech authorities offered no confirmation of his parents' deaths for quite some time, but he knew from Aunt Valda's letter that he could never expect their return. He was on his own, far from his homeland with his wife, only his young children to continue the ancient family line. I feel confident that my father, at that moment, vowed to fulfill Arnošt's last wish.

I recalled my brother's story about the day my dad died. His broken heart failed just two days after Mom died from the ravages of Parkinson's disease. At Dad's bedside, where my father lay conscious but eyes closed, Tom tried to say something that would help him feel good. Tom recounted his genealogical research. He noted that even though most of Arnošt and Olga's generation were murdered in the Holocaust, my father and other first cousins survived. He proudly reminded our father that he was the first Holzer born outside Bohemia in three hundred years. Finally, Tom said, "You won. You made it through the Holocaust and sprouted new branches on the family tree."

Suddenly and violently, without opening his eyes, my father shook his head back and forth, as if telling my brother, "No." Tom was surprised and puzzled by the reaction. Years later, I told Tom how the letters convinced me our father secretly carried a burden of survivor's guilt. We agreed it was apparent that he felt no "victory" in surviving. It was just life.

For two nights after reading my grandfather's final letter, which I have since named "The Letter that Changed Everything," I tossed and turned, staring into the darkness. I imagined my grandfather, this fine, gentle man sitting down at his desk in their small flat in Prague where the Nazis had forced them to move to congregate with other Jews. I could see him composing his last wishes for his only child and beloved son. Arnošt was a man who had fought in World War I and witnessed the nightmares and trauma that war inflicts on human beings. He expressed absolutely no fear for himself, only sorrow and concern for everyone else. Fulfilling their role of last will and testament, Arnošt's final words concentrated on respect and love for others. His wish—for his dear boy to use his skill as a doctor to "become a benefactor to the suffering humanity"—allowed me to fall in love with the grandfather I had never met.

As I read those words, I genuinely mourned my grandparents' death more than sixty years after their murder. It was an experience I can't fully explain. Not only did I realize I finally knew my grandfather to the depth of his soul, but I also longed for what my dad had called his father's "warm kisses." My heart was heavy with grief, and I felt overwhelming gloom that I would never have the chance to experience those kisses on my cheeks or forehead. Pure hatred robbed me and millions of others of this simple joy.

Mirek and Valli visited on Saturday to look over the rest of the letters and memorabilia, which stirred more profound sentiment. That night Derick left us to return to his home, adding dread to my emotional state—I have never been good at saying goodbye to my children when I know we will be apart for some time. After reading my grandfather's farewell letter, I kept wondering how my father felt, knowing that his son was gone.

My grandfather's letter was not just his goodbye and last wishes for my father—it was a communiqué from the Holocaust. His message was written for then, now, and forever. Not only for my father but all humanity, regardless of background or heritage.

The letter changed the course of my father's life. He had no doubt his parents were dead. Even as it caused grief and guilt, it had summoned him to live an extraordinarily compassionate future, honoring his father's wish. I'd witnessed my father fulfill the request.

The letter didn't only change the course of my dad's life; it transformed mine. I realized that words and stories stitch lives together in a meaningful mosaic that extends beyond every day, beyond the mundane. They remind us of what we believe in, memorialize, and instruct. Words encourage and provide hope to future generations. The stories we tell, the letters, emails, texts, and posts we write, the words we speak shape us. It became my turn to share my grandfather's wish with the world. My calling was to remind others that we each have an obligation for the common good to serve as benefactors to support others who need a helping hand or protection.

Arnošt with son Valdik, 1922

Steadfast Ink

Reading Dad's cache of correspondence and going through his other mementos was like time-traveling to a village in a far-off land inhabited by family, friends, and fascinating characters from my dad's past. The visit might have been an entirely enchanting experience if it hadn't been a village under siege.

This remarkable epistolary collection, written from the late 1930s through just after the Second World War, documented the fading hopes and desperation of a tight-knit community as their lives were crushed and shattered by mur-

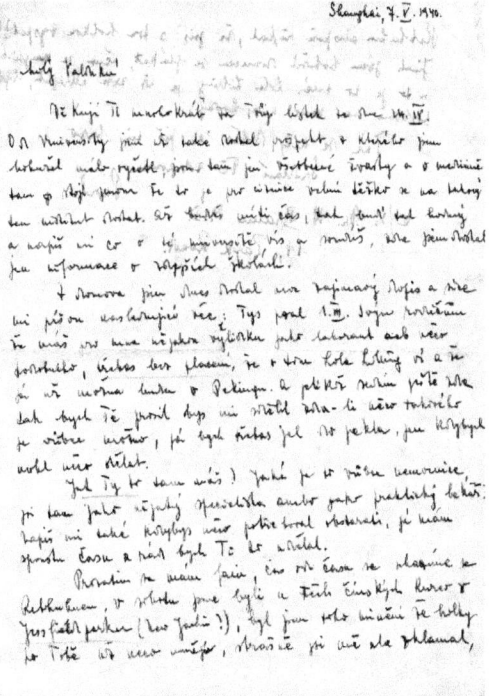

Pavel Kraus letter to Valdik, 1940

derous insanity. When their world as they knew it was gone, the communication stopped. As if their lives and place in history suddenly erased. One might think that meant the end. For me, it was the beginning.

I'm not ashamed to admit that I became obsessed with these letter writers. I came to view my father's correspondents as my friends. I felt their fears of forced displacement, their loneliness, and for some, pending death. I recoiled from their misfortunes. I took up the challenge of finding out what happened to all of them, even though I knew what I found might be awful. I relied on databases and websites easily accessed from my home computer, so my techniques weren't unique, but the results were.

Seventy-eight people, including my father, wrote some 400 letters that ended up stored in the two red lacquer boxes and other safe harbors. The letters were mailed from the Czech lands and Great Britain, France, Palestine, Sweden, Argentina, Ecuador, China, and the United States. A few were from addresses adrift, sent by passengers aboard ocean liners in dangerous wartime seas. Especially intriguing was the group of young, urban professionals—my father's friends and cousins—some of whom managed to escape Prague and others who were

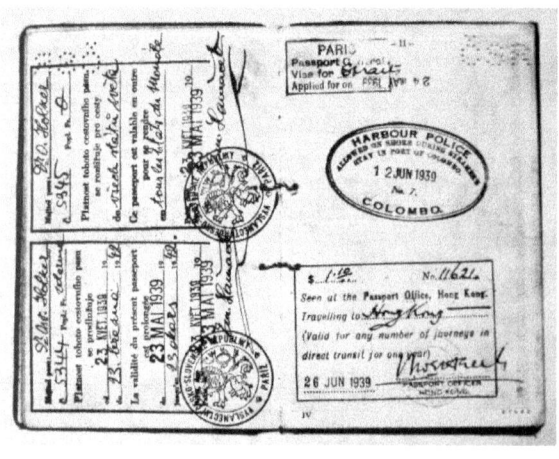

"Valdik" O. A. Holzer passport pages

trapped there. All of them were his worldwide correspondents. Each missive contained a piece of the life they'd left behind. It felt like a waterspout full of past truths spilling from the page into my present-day setting. Some held echoes reflected in current news reports about a desperate migrant crisis unfolding in the Mediterranean Sea or the United States' Southern border.

As I realized my journey of discovery was going to be a marathon, not a sprint, and the letter writers were no doubt now aged or dead, I began searching for several from the group. As I read and reread the mesmerizing translations, my lungs filled with their breath, and I wondered if some of these people were still breathing in real life.

Café Manes 1940

I learned of seven inseparable friends who regularly gathered in the 1930s with my father at Prague's Mánes Café. I located two still living and descendants of all the rest. I was so intrigued that I suspended drafting my dad's epic story (*My Dear Boy*) and took up writing another book—*Adventurers Against Their Will*. While there was still time, I delved into the seven correspondents' complete stories whose timeless lessons needed to be shared.

After nearly seventy years in storage, some of the paper used in letter writing had turned gray. Like the color of a faded Tiffany box exterior, a few still held a wisp of their original blue backgrounds. Depending on the ink used, I could easily read the contents or struggle to make out the words. I marveled over which Czech company had produced the most durable, steadfast ink.

Czech was the language of eighty percent of the letters. Once again, the translation was my biggest challenge. As I was growing up, my father taught me only a few select words in his native tongue—and most weren't appropriate for polite conversation.

When I began to work with the letters, I thought it was finally time for Czech language immersion; but I couldn't find any local classes. I accepted that this ancient Slavic language would not roll off my American tongue anytime soon. Closely related to Slovakian and Polish, Czech is unique because the religious martyr, Jan Hus, revised the spelling system in the 1400s. Hus introduced the *háček*, diacritical marks, and other accents that change a letter's pronunciation or stress. He created an alphabet containing twenty-seven letters when written without those marks but forty-two when written with them. Many Czech words carry a garbled cluster of consonants; an example is the word "*Mluvme*," which means, "Let's speak."

I took the first step by printing out the Czech words for the months of the year. Czechs don't have Latin-based names for their months. Dating from before the onset of Christianity, the Slavic calendar regards the months as seasonal changes in nature. I grew to love these foreign terms as I learned their meanings. *Leden* meant "the month of ice," or January. My favorite was May—*květen*, meaning "month of blooming flowers."

It was fascinating, but it would have been too time-consuming to learn a new language just to make sense of letters whose age and faded nature would have presented a challenge even if written in English. Unlike my linguistically adept father, who to some degree spoke eight languages—Czech, German, English, Chinese, Russian, French, Italian, Spanish—I was quick to throw in the towel, and yet, the puzzles were still there to be solved. Most were multi-page messages, written on paper of varying sizes and qualities, often brittle and yellowed with time. Usually, I could gently straighten the edge of a letter's first page, and the date, 1939 or 1941, would appear. But the tops of many sheets were frayed, sometimes making a date hard to decipher.

Luckily for me, the history I inherited wasn't all written in Czech. There were also lots of old pictures, postcards, and airmail envelopes bearing all sorts of stamps and seals. Dad saved many photographs

Escape Album cover, May – July 1939 photos

and documents that enhanced the stories told in the letters, like his faded aquamarine-blue leather album embossed with a dancing red

Chinese dragon—his "escape album." On the cover, he had affixed his fateful train ticket from when he'd fled Prague—its edges worn, but the letters "*y Wilsonova nád*" still decipherable. Presumably, the full phrase had been "*Československé státní dráhy Wilsonovo nádraží*" or Czechoslovak State Railways Wilson Station.

As I organized the material, I figured out how my father grouped some of the letters. He separated them by correspondent and interwove carbon copies of his type-written responses. On occasion, Dad kept everything in chronological order, essentially creating a dialogue from the past. Seven decades later, the United States Holocaust Memorial Museum's (USHMM) then Chief Archivist, Henry Mayer, told me this back and forth is very rare in an epistolary collection. Most of my father's seventy letters were duplicates—on extremely thin, now much-yellowed, onionskin. Sometimes, to conserve paper, he typed his second page on the reverse side, making the entire text almost impossible for the translator to decipher.

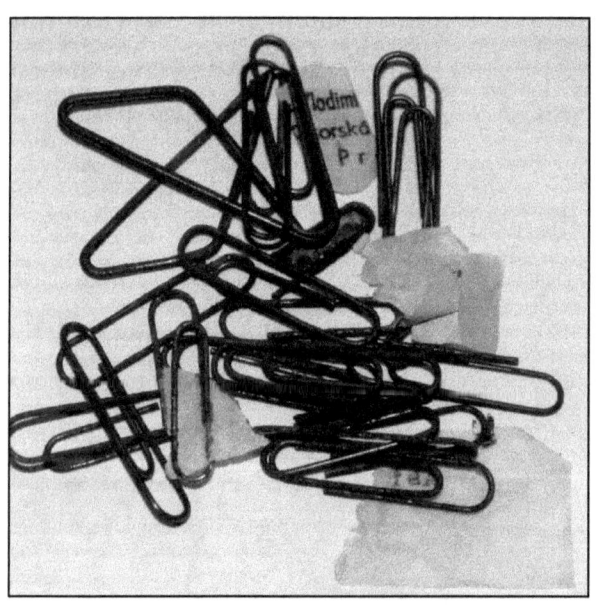

Rusty paperclips that held some letters together

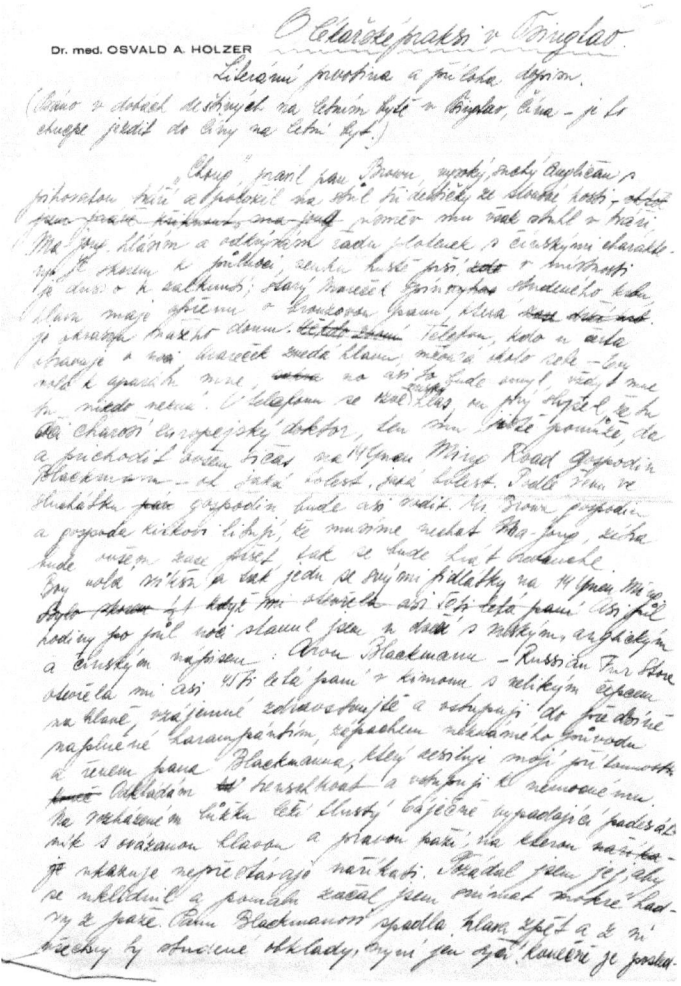

Valdik writing (N-1, Holzer Collection)

A few of his groupings spanned up to five years. When translated, I recognized, these letters would allow me to get to know my young father in a way I never had before. By overhearing his conversations during his formative years from twenty-six to thirty-one, I'd meet the man my mom was about to fall in love with! His letters covered the period when he'd fled the Nazis in Prague, traveled the world, met my mother in China, and begun his family and career. It was like finding an old camera, lost for decades, which contained a roll of film with photographs of my young dad. If I could develop the film, the images would be mine. To do so, I had to enter the darkroom.

How Schindler's List Led to Valdik's List

Valdik Holzer, Czechoslovak Army, 1938

Several years after my teenage joyride fiasco, I got a real taste of my father's Czech temper. At the age of twenty, I quit college at Florida State University and eloped with my high school boyfriend,

Rick Schirm. When I phoned home with the news, Mom helped calm my father down, as she always did, but not before he declared, "I've been kicked once in my life. I won't be kicked again by my own daughter." At the time, I didn't know the full details of the Nazi "kick" he'd endured and wondered why he was so hard on me. When I replay the event now through the lens of our family history, I understand how I let him down.

Not only were his own academic achievements a source of great pride, but he also believed education helped him survive and succeed in a world he could never take for granted. It hurt him that I'd quit school. He worried that I was making a terrible mistake. It didn't take long for either of us to get over being grouchy, and I was as determined as my father had been to succeed through hard work.

It took me a few years to settle into the right career path as a non-engineer woman in the business of engineering, but I did search for and follow it with all the energy and commitment that both my father and mother had handed down to me. Dad may not have agreed with my academic exit choice, but I took great satisfaction in his pride in my successes. Years later, he seemed almost as thrilled with my career as I was when the impossible came true in March 1992. As a result of the volunteer effort I'd spearheaded, the Fédération Internationale de Football Association (FIFA) chose Orlando to host five soccer matches for the 1994 World Cup. I was the only women bid, and host chair FIFA had ever encountered in their worldwide extravaganzas. Chosen as one of nine USA host cities, we were the smallest market. Working with four thousand enthusiastic volunteers, I had to tend to a million details to ensure everything was in place for a world-class event. In the end, the

Atlanta Constitution named Orlando "the best venue in the best World Cup ever."

I also had to tend to the not-so-small detail of making a living. The company I worked for was sold to a much larger corporation, and I was laid off along with other longtime managers. Luckily, my golden handcuffs agreement allowed my stock shares to be redeemed for a new future. At age forty-three, I took on the challenge of starting my own Orlando engineering firm with three former colleagues. Adding to the stress was the end of my marriage: I was now a single mom with my daughter Kelly in college and my son Derick in elementary school.

Of course, I still made time for the hour-long drive to visit my folks as often as possible. By now, they'd sold our riverside home and moved into their seaside condo as an accommodation to their empty nest and advancing years. Later the one-level condo would prove more comfortable for Mom to navigate as her Parkinson's disease progressed. In 1992, I remarried. Roger Neiswender, my dear and supportive husband for the second half of my life, grew to love my parents as much as they loved him.

All was going well until I overstepped the bounds of our special father-daughter rapport during a visit to their condo. Like nearly everyone else in America in 1993, I'd read about a new film called *Schindler's List*, an epic historical drama directed and produced by Steven Spielberg about a Sudeten German businessman who helped save many of his Jewish factory workers from the Holocaust. Oskar Schindler was an ethnic German and Catholic who came from Svitavy, in Moravia (a part of the Czech lands). Schindler served in the Czechoslovak Army, attaining in 1938 the rank of lance corporal in the reserves. He took advantage of the German program to "Aryanize" Jewish-owned companies by acquiring one in occupied Poland. I thought my father could identify with the film's theme and hoped that seeing it might encourage him to talk about his family's experience. In what must have been a lapse in my sanity, I asked him if he'd like to go to the movie with me.

As his bushy eyebrows pinched together, pain struck his eighty-two-year-old face from eyebrows to chin. He slowly rose from his seat across the dining table from my mother and me. When he reached his full height, he spoke in his loud, deep voice with its resonating Czech accent: "No. I will not go with you. It is not a movie that I intend to see . . . ever!"

The memory of my white-haired father, his eyes welling with tears, will remain with me always. I felt an overwhelming sorrow and knew I should say nothing more. But from that moment, my childhood bond transformed into a grown-up one as I began to discover my real father. Later that evening, we sat together—just the two of us—as he finally pried from his heart the memories of the most painful time in his life. I stayed by his side as he used his old Voss typewriter to slowly record the names of the forty-four relatives who had perished in the Holocaust. He also listed the names of those who had survived and spent the war in Nazi slave labor camps.

I've called it Valdik's List ever since.

Marie Holzer . . . Ernest (Arnošt) Holzer . . . Olga Holzer . . . Rudolph Winternitz . . . Olga Winternitz . . . Gustav Steiner . . . Erna Steiner . . . Lilly Steiner . . . Hana Steiner . . . Jakub Furth . . . Regina Furth . . .

Name after name appeared in black letters—his grandmother, parents, uncles, aunts, cousins. I was shocked. Until that moment, I knew my father had lost three family members in the Holocaust. I'd never known the scope or the details. These were secrets he'd guarded for nearly a half-century. He might never have shared them if I hadn't been foolish enough to ask if he'd like to see a movie that I now know featured a powerful scene in which human ash from incinerators burning the dead falls like snow from the sky. Never forget.

Valdik's List

As he typed, Dad created a code to explain relationships—"A" for aunt, "O" for an uncle, "GA" for great-aunt, and so on. With the surnames grouped together, it became clear that the victims had disappeared from his father's and mother's families in almost equal numbers. When he thought he knew how and where someone had died, he wrote the name of the concentration camp—"TZ" for Terezín or "A" for Auschwitz—and added the year of death, almost always 1942. Next to the names of some of the aunts or uncles, like Arthur Porges, he added a notation such as "Family of 4, A." This code was indicating that the entire family was murdered at

Auschwitz. For survivors, such as his Aunt Valerie "Valda" Mařík and several cousins, he wrote what he knew of their circumstances. Under the heading "3rd Generation," he added his name:

Oswald Holzer left Prague on May 21, 1939, for China & the USA

My father never revealed how he had gathered all this information or how he felt about the enormous tragedy. We didn't speak; he typed with two fingers as I watched and swallowed tears. When he finished, Dad penciled in a few Czech diacriticals on appropriate characters as if offering an ultimate sign of respect.

That was as far as my father was able to travel emotionally because the past scarred him in a way that I had never known nor could have comprehended at the time. My mind drifted to this revelation about my paternal family history. Say this aloud: *"Forty-four of my relatives were murdered. My grandpa, my grandma, my great-grandma, great-aunts, great-uncles, cousins..."*

Imagine. I was forty-five years old and just learning forty-four members of my family tree were murdered—gassed, shot, starved, or beaten to death—because of sheer hatred. I was still fifteen years away from my research which revealed the tremendous pain Dad's story holds. I was also still fifteen years away from discovering the breathtaking gift that my grandfather bestowed on his son. My grandfather Arnošt presented him with a wish for his life that ensured Dad would not be consumed with grief or revenge but find a purpose of giving to others during his life.

Like the sudden heat of a humid Florida breeze through a newly opened window, the immense grief my father had lived with enveloped me. It may be hard to understand how a daughter so close to her dad could not have known the darkest truths of his past. I never pushed him for information about what happened during the war; if he wanted to tell me more, he would. In our family, we lived our joy-filled American lives, always focusing on the present and future. It turns out that when I thought I'd learned everything there was to know about my family, I was just beginning.

Looking to the East

Fifteen years later, the more I pored over the correspondence, the more I hungered for an understanding of my grandparents' final days. By the end of April 2008, after I had placed all the letters in protective plastic sleeves, I reached out to a trustworthy source to help me understand what happened in Arnošt and Olga's world as they faced their final journey.

I wrote to Peter Black, Ph.D., Senior Historian of the United States Holocaust Memorial Museum (USHMM) in Washington, DC, and told him about the letters. I shared what I'd learned from the International Tracing Service (now Arolsen Archives). On April 24, 1942, my grandparents were passengers 530 and 531 on Nazi Transport Am from Prague to Terezín in the northwest area of today's Czech Republic. On May 25, 1942, they were sent "to the east" as passengers 906 and 907 on Transport Az. By then, I was acquainted with the phrase "to the east," a Nazi code for sending Jews and many others the Nazis deemed "undesirables" to camps in German-occupied Eastern Poland.

Nazi transport records (Arolsen Archives): Arnošt and Olga (Orlik) Holzer, April 24 and May 25, 1942

I knew from my research that my eighty-year-old great-grandmother, Marie (née Porges) Holzer, died in Terezín of pneumonia. Subsequent investigation revealed she was passenger 588 on the Bd transport on September 4, 1942. Her life ended on December 26, 1942. I told Peter I wasn't sure where my grandparents perished. My father's stories and research led me to guess it might have been Auschwitz-Birkenau or Majdanek concentration camps in Poland.

DEM SONDERSTANDESAMT VORGELEGT   Datum:

Name: HOLZER-OVA, Marie
geboren am 8.3.1862 in   -   Nat.
gestorben am 26.12.1942 in Theresienstadt
Todesursache
beerdigt am .... in ....

STERBEURKUNDE Nr. 1854 Ast.I. (Stempel)   Datum 1978
ausgestellt aufgrund folgender Dokumente
            Sonderstandesamt
            Arolsen, Kreis Waldeck

Copy in conformity with the ITS archives

Nazi death record from Arolsen Archives: Marie (Porges) Holzer, December 26, 1942, Theresienstadt (Terezin)

Within a week, Peter contacted me by telephone. His voice was deep and tone authoritative as he conveyed the museum's interest in being the repository of the Holzer collection so the information could be available to scholars worldwide. He shared his knowledge of the Nazi transports and speculated on the details of my grandparents' last journey.

"It is not possible to know with great certainty what happened to your grandparents, but I think I can tell you a little more than you know now and lead you to some additional sources which might be helpful." Peter began telling me about the particular Az transport on May 25, 1942, that carried a few Czechs but primarily Austrian and

German Jews from Terezín to the "Lublin District" in eastern Poland. Realizing this conversation wasn't going to be easy, I took a seat in my living room overlooking our tranquil lake.

I knew that my grandparents' demise in the spring of 1942 was intertwined with the early implementation of Hitler's horrendous "Final Solution of the Jewish Problem." But Peter started talking about something I wasn't familiar with—a Nazi procedural plan identified by the code name "Operation Reinhard," or in German, *Aktion Reinhard*. He said it mainly represented the detail and goals for how the genocide would be carried out.

Referencing an authoritative source, Peter said it was likely that my grandparents were taken directly from the main train center in German-occupied Lublin, Poland, to a killing camp such as Sobibor or Belzec. These were two of the three centers built by the Nazis under Operation Reinhard for the singular purpose of mass murder (the third being Treblinka). Peter suggested that I research the exact train schedules to learn if more information could be found, but he guessed that my grandparents were taken to Sobibor, a place I had never heard of until Peter mentioned it.

Peter went on to say there was a remote chance that fifty-six-year-old Arnošt if he appeared healthy and younger than his age, could have been conscripted into forced labor at Lublin's Majdanek concentration camp, but it wasn't likely. Most of the forced laborers were in their twenties and thirties. Had Arnošt been chosen, he would probably have succumbed to starvation, disease, exposure, or other brutality as he performed harsh physical labor under brutal conditions.

Feeling a lump grow in my throat, I asked if my grandparents would have been together as this final journey unfolded. There was more to learn before the answer came. According to Peter, once given summons in Prague by the Jewish Religious Congregation that stated the day and hour of transport departure, they would have gathered in an area known as the Trade Fair Grounds near Stromovka Park. A barbed-wire site with a few decrepit barracks was where previously, the radio industry annually displayed the new developments in their field. There were no sanitary facilities except for outdoor latrines located quite a distance away.

Guarded by Czech police outside and SS units inside, Arnošt and Olga were likely forced to sleep in a shack on filthy mattresses, their suitcase, or the ground. After turning in their ration cards, house keys, and valuables, they were probably summoned for transport before dawn or late at night to avoid a public spectacle. From there, they were taken to the Holešovice-Bubny train station.

"They may have been able to ride the train together in challenging conditions," Peter said. Being the early stages of the Nazi initiative, they may have been in crowded passenger cars rather than cattle cars. "When they arrived at the District Lublin, if they were taken to one of the killing centers, they may again have traveled there together. Once in the place, with no housing, their fate was quickly carried out."

Peter told me there wasn't much of a paper trail for prisoners unless they managed to survive. From a letter I received in 2004 from the International Red Cross International Tracing Service (ITS), now Arolsen Archives, in Bad Arolsen, Germany, it was evident part of the information relied on a May 1951 letter written by the Czechoslovak Red Cross of Prague.

That letter reported, "It can be gathered that the Transport Az is to be considered a death transport since fewer than ten percent of the 1,000 deportees returned home after the war." It also included two excerpts from Terezín documents that contained all the information available in 1951 about my grandparents' incarceration—two index cards with handwritten notes listing their names, birthdates, Prague residence address, and the date of transport. Since the time of the Czechoslovak Red Cross letter, Peter said additional sources of information might have become available at the museum sites at Majdanek, Terezín, or Sobibor, where a small museum existed.

When I hung up the telephone, I sat in solitude, looking out the window at the reflection of the billowy clouds over our lake, wondering about this place called Sobibor. I visited the Holocaust Museum's website, searching under "Lublin/Majdanek."

Disturbing facts on my screen revealed the methodical blueprint for murder:

Operation Reinhard, named after Reinhard Heydrich, head of the German Reich Security Main Office, was the detailed plan for the Nazi's Final Solution. It was implemented under SS Major General supervision between October 1941 and November 1943 and had four goals:

- ❖ The physical annihilation of the Jews residing in the German-controlled territory.
- ❖ The exploitation of some Jews selected to survive temporarily as forced laborers.

- ❖ The seizure, evaluation, and recycling of clothing, personal property, valuables, and currency taken from the murdered Jews at the killing centers.
- ❖ The identification and securing of so-called hidden assets of the Jewish population.

Three killing centers—Belzec, Sobibor, and Treblinka II—were constructed for the sole purpose of killing Jews.

The mass slaughter proceeded with blinding swiftness and brutal results: Between March and June 1942, about fourteen thousand Jews from Bohemia and Moravia arrived in Lublin. The SS sent most of them to Izbica and Piaski. In these ghettos, Jews were held temporarily while awaiting further deportation and then directly to Sobibor when it was ready in May.

By November 1942, Operation Reinhard had killed approximately 1.7 million Jews, including 250,000 at Sobibor. Stop and think about that—*one million seven hundred thousand people murdered*. Grandfathers, grandmothers, sisters, uncles, mothers, fathers, children.

Constructed in a wooded swamp near the Bug River, along a railway line near the small village of Sobibor, the camp was in the eastern sector of the Lublin district, near Ukraine. After its completion in the early spring of 1942, the Nazis executed 61,400 Jews in the first three months. In all likelihood, Arnošt and Olga Holzer were among them.

I read testimony from the Nuremberg Trials to learn the painful truth describing how the extermination process operated. It left me

Transports from Terezin ("Theresienstadt") and Prague - Destinations

Last Update 2 June 2006

Transports from "Protektorat Böhmen und Mähren" (Theresienstadt and Prag) to the General Gouvernement and the Reinhard camps (Copyright: Peter Witte 10.10.2002).

Transport	Date	Destination	Number of Persons	Final Destination	Survivors
Aa	11/03/1942	Izbica - KZ Lublin	1003	Belzec, Sobibor	7
Ab	17/03/1942	Izbica - KZ Lublin	1000	Belzec, Sobibor	3
Ag	01/04/1942	Piaski - KZ Lublin	1008	Sobibor	5
Ap	18/04/1942	Rejowiec- KZ Lublin	1000	Sobibor	3
Al	23/04/1942	KZ Lublin(400)-Piaski(600)	1000	Sobibor	1
An	25/04/1942	Warsaw	1000	Treblinka	7
Aq	27/04/1942	KZ Lublin(400)-Izbica(600)	1000	Belzec, Sobibor	1
Ar	28/04/1942	Zamosc	1000	Belzec, Sobibor	5
As	30/04/1942	Zamosc	1000	Belzec, Sobibor	
Ax	09/05/1942	KZ Lublin - Siedliszcze	1000	Sobibor	
Ay	17/05/1942	KZ Lublin(400)-Kr. Chelm(600)	1000	Sobibor	
Az	25/05/1942	KZ Lublin-Ujazdow	1000	Sobibor	1
Aah from Prague	10/06/1942	KZ Lublin-Ujazdow	1000	Sobibor	2
Aak	12/06/1942	KZ Lublin-Sawin	1000	Sobibor	12
Aai	13/06/1942	KZ Lublin (Sobibor?)	1000	Sobibor	
Bo	19/09/1942	Treblinka	2000		
Bp	21/09/1942	Treblinka	2020		
Bq	23/09/1942	Treblinka	1980		
Br	26/09/1942	Treblinka	2004		
Bs	29/09/1942	Treblinka	2000		
Bt	05/10/1942	Treblinka	1000		
Bu	08/10/1942	Treblinka	1000		Glazar, Unger
Bv	15/10/1942	Treblinka	1984		
Bw	19/10/1942	Treblinka	2000		
Bx	22/10/1942	Treblinka	2018		

Transport List (from Theresienstadt/Terezin to Lublin to Sobibor, Az)

sick to my stomach. In *Ghetto Theresienstadt* by Zdeněk Lederer, I realized that only "one prisoner" survived the Az transport to which Arnošt and Olga were assigned. Because he was a watchmaker, that prisoner was sent to Auschwitz and put to work. "On February 18, 1943, he was transferred to concentration camp Sachsenhausen-Oranienburg where he stayed until April 1945. On the death march of the prisoners of this camp, he reached the Baltic Sea, where he was liberated."

I now had confirmation that my grandfather was not the fortunate one: he was not a watchmaker. He'd inherited his family wholesale grocery business in Benešov. And, while my father attended medical school at Prague's Charles University, his parents had moved to Prague where, according to papers I found, Arnošt worked as a 'business representative.' Unlike the fortunate watchmaker, I now had proof that grandfather Arnošt, who I was robbed of ever knowing, never saw the sea again.

I tried to envision my grandparents' last hours. I believe at the time they boarded the Az transport, Arnošt suspected that death awaited him, and Olga aged fifty-four. The Nazi charade never fooled him. I envisioned how he tried to protect his wife from anticipating that reality. I cannot fathom the terror they felt as they walked naked toward the gas chambers of Sobibor down the narrow path diabolically named by the Nazis: *Himmelfahrtstrasse* or "Street to Heaven."

My grandparents must have thought about my father and how much they loved him, imagining kisses on his forehead. They had not been able to hug their only child goodbye. Their last sight of him had been precisely three years earlier in the Prague railway station as the puffing smoke from his train wafted around them. That day, with tears running down her cheeks, my grandmother began her death march. She just didn't know it.

Olga with son Valdik, circa 1915

What Was Known

China, July 1939, Shanghai harbor under Japanese control,
Photo by Valdik Holzer

After my father escaped from his Nazi-occupied Czech homeland and, using a black market visa, arrived in Shanghai in July 1939, he discovered a world far different from any he'd ever experienced. My favorite research topic for my books included learning about China's role in my father's life. From the seven hours of interviews I did with Dad, many of them about China, I learned a lot of what the country meant to him. Most of the letters he saved were correspondence he received or wrote while he was there. His love affair with my mother began in China, the background for the most heartwarming and spicy scenes in my second book, *My Dear Boy*.

Overrun with some 20,000 other Jews who fled to Shanghai, this unlikely port of refuge in the late 1930s and early 40s differed from others globally, as most countries closed their borders to desperate Jewish refugees. The Japanese controlled Shanghai's port and parts of the city as they battled to increase their occupation of critical areas of China. For a short window of time, the Japanese required no visas or entry permits, and thus Shanghai became an unlikely attainable destination.

I realized it was a complex challenge in China for European immigrants to learn the truth of unfolding violent circumstances back home before and during World War II. One primary source of information in Shanghai was the rabidly anti-British German-sponsored radio station XGRS (GRS for German Radio Station) set up in 1940 in the German Concession. In letters home, my father reported the unreliability of their news reports. The 'concessions' existed during late Imperial China and the Republic of China, governed and occupied by foreign powers. It was a form of international relations in unequal treaties, where China transferred public functions and rights to various foreign governments to operate these concessions. British, American, and French citizens enjoyed extraterritorially and consular jurisdiction. Most had their own newspapers attempting to share news from home and Shanghai's happenings. The international settlement came to a close in December 1941 when the Japanese troops took over after the Pearl Harbor attack.

When Germany fell in 1945, its ally Japan seized the radio station. When Japan fell too, the station went to the Chinese and became the only shortwave station to remain on the air in Shanghai after the war.

Chilling questions filled my being as I watched old videos of the shocking images of dead bodies in piles from German concentration and death camps. Those who survived in mostly skeletal forms came into focus, horrifying humanity, which at last realized what humans were capable of doing to other humans.

When did the United States government realize the full extent of the Nazi violence? I found the answer on the United States Holocaust Memorial Museum website (here paraphrased from "The United States and The Holocaust")[3]:

> *Intelligence data and news reports revealed Nazi violence against Jews as early as 1933. Even though there was a dramatic increase in that violence in 1941, scholars generally agree that the United States government did not receive reliable confirmation of the full scope of the Nazi's "Final Solution" until August 1942* [three months after Arnošt and Olga perished at Sobibor].
>
> *On August 1, 1942, Gerhart Riegner, a representative of the World Jewish Congress in Switzerland, received information from a German source regarding a Nazi plan to exterminate all the Jews in Europe. Due to the report's shocking and somewhat unbelievable nature, Riegner refrained from passing on this information until he investigated its source. One week later, satisfied with the reliability of the informant—though*

---

[3] https://www.ushmm.org/collections/bibliography/the-united-states-and-the-holocaust

unable to confirm the news itself—Riegner requested that the American consulate in Geneva cable this information to the American and other Allied governments and the American Jewish Leader, Stephen Wise, President of the World Jewish Congress. The US State Department failed to pass the report on to Wise, but that same month he received the report via British channels. Wise was asked by the US for more time for its sources to seek confirmation. Three months later, they said they had it.

Poster by Czech artist and Valdik friend, Adolf Hoffmeister, in exile, New York City, 1943

In the months that followed the initial message, as reports of massacres of Jews steadily increased, a pile of evidence also grew validating the idea that the Nazis were carrying out a plan to destroy the Jews of Europe. Finally, on November 24, 1942, Rabbi Wise held a press conference (in New York City) to announce news of the Nazis' "extermination campaign." A few weeks later, on December 17, 1942, the United States, Britain, and ten other allied governments made this news official, feeling confident enough in the evidence to reveal their knowledge of the Nazi plan to systemically kill all of Europe's Jews publicly. They released a formal declaration confirming and condemning Hitler's extermination policy toward the Jews.

The press conference took place just three months after my parents had left New York City for Lafayette, Indiana, where my dad became a doctor for Home Hospital. The non-profit hospital, a division of Sisters of St. Francis Health Services, was known as "the Home for Friendless," a place where care was provided to homeless residents.

How widely was the information about the atrocities committed on Jews covered in the 1942 print or radio media? There was no social media. Would my parents have read about it in Lafayette, Indiana's local newspaper? Most likely not. The *New York Times*, for example, allocated space on the front page for only the latter of these official reports, relegating Wise's press conference to page ten. Most major dailies in the United States minimized the event's importance by burying it on their inner pages.

I found clues and revelations in the cache of letters. For example, through correspondence my dad received after the war, he made assumptions of where family members perished. My follow-up research showed that my dad received information about the concentration camps that weren't accurate. It was sometimes second-hand information or rumor. If he had gone looking for official documents, it would have been a challenging search. With its vast archives, the United States Holocaust Memorial Museum didn't open until 1993. Nazi records from seventy years ago are still being released, often now digitally, to the waiting public worldwide by Arolsen Archives (formerly the ITS) in Bad Arolsen, Germany, which makes me appreciate the legacy of the Chinese red lacquer boxes even more.

I often speculate about what my father envisioned would happen when his letters were discovered after his death. Did he worry that the collection wouldn't be recognized for its extraordinary personal and moral value or its meaning for the world?

Then, I think of the optimistic man he was, and I'm convinced he knew it would all come together as it has.

For my high school graduation present in June 1966, my grandmother Emma (née Kroeger) Lequear gave me a copy of the book *Markings* by Dag Hammarskjöld. The famous Swedish diplomat and Secretary of the United Nations described his diary reflections as a "sort of White Book concerning my negotiations with myself and with God." On page 58, I highlighted the following:

> *The longest journey*
> *Is the journey inwards.*
> *Of him who has chosen his destiny,*
> *Who has started upon his quest*
> *For the source of his being.*

Fifty years after my grandmother imprinted this insightful man's words on my being, I realize Hammarskjöld's wisdom still holds true. My longest and the most consequential journey has been the journey inward.

My Czech Grandparents' Epitaph

"*Only endless longing remains in the heart...*"
OLGA HOLZER, to Valdik, March 3, 1942, one month before receiving the Nazi transport order, and sent via a cousin living in a neutral country: Argentina.

Throughout my childhood, I knew my missing Czech grandparents only as the man and woman in the sepia-toned photograph on Dad's dresser.

I had seen it countless times—stared at it. I can still describe the image from memory: likely taken in their Prague apartment, husband and wife stand close to each other behind a floral fabric couch. Their elegant clothes look timeless. My round-faced grandmother wears a black dress with the top showcasing exquisite lace in the shape of a black vine embracing her shoulders. A delicate strand of white pearls peeks out from around her neck. Her hair is dark and cut short. My balding grandfather wears a dark suit, white shirt, and a gray tie. Both seemed surrounded by an aura of light. The seriousness of the photo, circa 1941, was betrayed only by the slightest Mona Lisa smile on each of my grandparents' faces. Now I know my grandmother wore little jewelry because, by that time, they'd hidden her most precious belongings, buried in an orchard to elude Nazi confiscation.

The closer I looked, the more I could identify our family resemblance. I could see my father's features: his sturdy nose, luminous eyes, thin lips, and heart-shaped face. Dad was a mixture of his parents' DNA, just as I reflect my mother and him in my smile, eyes, and hair color. The barrel shape of my father's arms resembled his mother's. Dad's distinctive broad hands, made for the perfect surgeon, with fingers almost all the same length, were an exact match to his father's hand resting gracefully on the floral couch.

I shared a connection to these people, but I felt no emotion when I looked at that photograph. I'd never met them and believed I never would because they had been murdered in a Nazi death camp six years before I was born.

Yet, in a profound sense, I did finally meet them. I have since come to know and love them—through the letters that my father kept hidden along with his feelings. As I read their words of concern and advice, of struggle under the fist of the Nazis, my grandparents transformed from images in photographs to real people who were very much my family. The longer I researched, the more I treasured this beautiful, emotional experience, holding immense sorrow and joy all at once. Although I never heard their voices, when I met my other Czech relatives still living in the Czech Republic, I listened to them in a whole new manner. I felt a sense of purpose in uncovering my grandparents' true nature.

This feeling of purpose propelled my odyssey and sustained me

Antique Chinese Box

as I—with the help of translators and other experts—got down to the exhausting work of organizing and ultimately making sense of my father's letter collection. None of it was more important or meaningful to me than the forty-four letters from my grandparents, who became increasingly real and loving with each translated sentence. The correspondence in the red lacquer boxes from Arnošt and Olga began on October 14, 1940, five days before my parents' wedding in China, following their whirlwind six weeks of courtship. Most of their letters are addressed not singularly to my father but to "*Drahé děti*," meaning "Dear Children." I have no definitive explanation for why there were no letters preserved from Arnošt and Olga when my father departed his homeland from 1939 to the fall of 1940. It seems serendipitous that the letters that survived date from the moment my dad was no longer alone. My mother, who served as my father's shining beacon for the remainder of his days, was joyfully included in the most critical letters he hid away. There is a Yiddish expression that is very fitting here: *Bashert*. It means destined or fated, and it is often used in the context of marriage to describe a true soulmate. As I examined my Jewish roots, I often learned new words that matched the moment at hand. When I think about my parents' perfect pairing, beyond Bashert, a Hebrew phrase—*Tikkun Olam*—describes their actions well. Tikkun Olam represents acts of kindness performed to mend or repair the world. As a benefactor, my father was consumed with helping heal the sick, and the phrase reflects my mother's selfless, unwavering commitment to bring and sustain peace and love in our world.

The first dispatch from Arnošt was written on his old business letterhead from "Benešov u Prahy," indicating Benešov's proximity to the cosmopolitan city. Until I read this letter, I did not know of Arnošt's enterprises' diversity. This one referenced "Auto Supplies—The Patent Vehicle Elevator" along with "Petrol—Diesel—Auto Oils and Tires." From my father's taped interview I did in 1989, it was clear that Dad shared his love of automobiles with his father. Reading the letter, I realized beyond pleasure, it was evident that there was a business side to Arnošt's attachment.

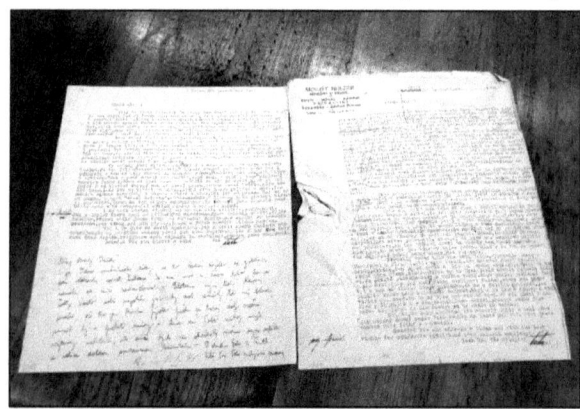

Arnošt and Olga sample letters

I think the following letter, one of the earliest I have, is a perfect representation of Arnošt and Olga's spirit and resilience. You don't have to know anything about the friends and relatives whose names pop up in the banalest reference. I didn't recognize many of them until I'd done months of laborious puzzle-solving on the more than 300 names mentioned in the letter collection. What's important is that their inclusion is proof that my grandparents were trying to carry on everyday life, to sustain the back-and-forth of gossip and good cheer under increasingly harsh conditions and uncertainty about the future. It's impossible to know how much of their resolve is genuine and how much is theater for my father's sake, but I'm not sure it matters. These were remarkable people who did the world a great service by documenting the times they were forced to live.

> Arnošt Holzer
> Praha XII (#61)
> Slezská 127 December 18, 1940
>
> Dear children!
> On Monday, the letter no. 37 from the 18th of this month arrived and then right the following day the letter no. 38, so as can be seen, the mail comes much faster and regularly to us than to you. We still have not missed any of your letters, and we hope that even the two letters you still haven't received will surely soon arrive in addition.

Due to the convoluted and unreliable routes that the mail traveled, Arnošt took to numbering his communications. This system was to keep track of which letters reached their destinations and perhaps their arrival time. Within the seventy carbon copies of my father's saved letters, I do not have copies from my father to his parents, so I will never know how well Arnošt's system worked. When Arnošt wrote from Prague to Los Angeles in 1941, his letters may have gone first to Vienna for censorship, through Switzerland, and then "via Siberia-Tokio-Pacific." This route is shown on one of the saved envelopes in my father's stamp collection books. Sometimes Arnošt used as many as six stamps to support the long trip.

> As the Fischers recently learned, Erny with Tomík are supposed to have left already for the USA. At the same time, Rudla supposedly stays temporarily with several friends near Hanička and is doing well. It is nonetheless still strange that he hasn't written to you for so long since, based on past correspondence, it was apparent that you had a lively exchange. Let's hope that you have learned a bit more in the meantime and that in one of your next letters, we will find some mention of it. The Winternitzes are receiving, again and again, satisfactory news from Franzl and are therefore calm. You see what an advantage you have when you can see some nice films and in this way see what's new. That we have not experienced for more than five quarters of a year. So you have again seen at least one acquaintance with whom you left here . . .
>
> Let's hope that your efforts managed to chase out Dr. Weinstein's gallstones without surgery. Aren't you lucky to win five whole USA dollars! That isn't such a staggering amount, but for some good dinner, it should have been sufficient. We can imagine how you made a night of it. Mom keeps racking her brain about how much such Japanese pearls would cost here, and so indeed, she will place a question with several jewelers to estimate how much you untied your purse-strings for that wedding present. We wish our dear Ruth that she will continue to have such luck with hunting for those pearls and not only with

this choice but also with all other choices in life.

We are very happy that both of you accepted our little shipment of sheet music with such gratitude, and I would have repeated it immediately had I already had the response to the letter mailed together with that parcel. I hope you will write to me what dear Ruth would like from what I suggested to send some more sheet music as a little belated Christmas present. We thank her very much for her kind letter. We hope you translate our letters for her since they are naturally intended for both of you. I don't want to write in English today until I learn how that first attempt at expressing emotions in English ended up sounding, if it weren't a farce, since as I already wrote to you in my first such letter, "I will not lose face" in the eyes of my new daughter. So next time I will thank you in some good English. Of course, I understand her letters well, and I impart their contents to Mom.

The other news concerning your wardrobe greatly comforted us. We were apprehensive about it since the possible loss of clothes would certainly smite you very palpably. Regarding the other things, I already noted in one of the last letters that now we only select parts of the news, as we have learned to read newspapers much better. Nonetheless, we see that even you aren't certain about your stay and that in the end, you have turned for advice to America, where they will be able to get good advice. We are therefore looking forward to your next news with great interest. You would undoubtedly find many friends, and should you go through San Francisco, stop by Epstein and give him my regards. He is behaving very nicely to all those émigrés.

Practical Physician will not be delivered in the New Year. The subscription is paid until then . . .

In one of the last letters, I also mentioned that we borrowed Rudla's record player. The machine plays very nicely, and Rudla had lovely records too, mostly modern dance and only about two records with opera excerpts. I gave myself an excellent present for Christmas. I bought myself Smetana's "From My Life," performed by a Czech quartet. You may imagine that I listen to it with passion and how often I play it. Similarly, in turn, you probably listen to the beautiful melodies of Dvořák's Slavonic Dances, the Moldau, and Bohemian Fields and Groves. Only I wonder whether you manage to set the right pace for dear Ruth.

Well, I don't really have any more to write to you. Today, Lenda {Uncle Leo Holzer} reported that he too got a New Year's greeting from you. Since Mother immediately put it with all the other trophies of yours, it somehow escaped my accounting, and thus I only now remember it. My sincere thanks, and as I already wrote you, we wish you also a Happy New Year and Merry Christmas.

Wholehearted greetings and kisses.

Yours,

Dad

Enclosed was this note from Olga:

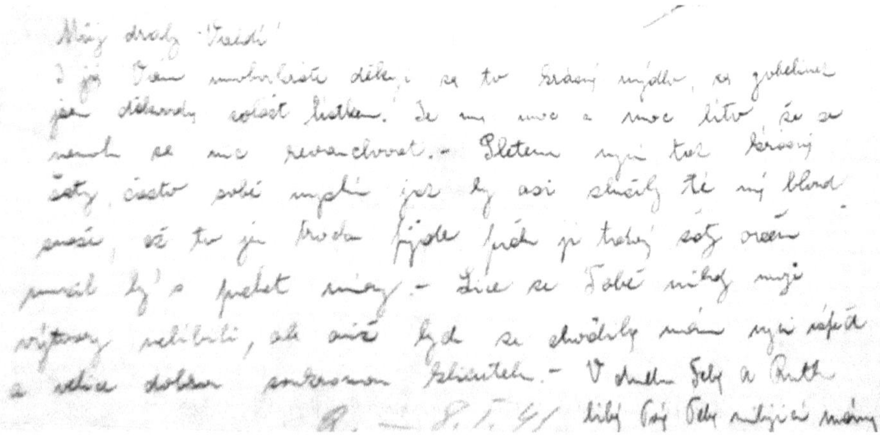

Olga sample handwriting

My dear Valdi!

I just returned from town, so this pre-Christmas bustle in the streets reminded me of the times we often spent together and how you always liked Prague before Christmas and those sales.

All is the same, only the Těsnohlídek's Christmas tree[4] is missing. So I am often with you in spirit; you are surely celebrating beautiful Christmas. You always wanted and liked the true Catholic Christmas, so now your wish has come close to fulfillment. I am delighted that you so often think of me with gifts but believe me that I am no longer that vain. I have no other wishes than just to see you once again. In my mind, kissing you and Ruth.

Your loving Mom

I wonder how my father interpreted his parents' mostly positive tone. He claimed to keep up as best he could with Prague events through friends, travelers, and whatever news sources were available in China. I'm unsure how much he knew then about the actions taken by the Protectorate's government in the months before this letter was written. According to material in the United States Holocaust Memorial Museum archives, the degradation of Jewish rights was far-reaching and unending from the time my father left Prague:

- ❖ Jews were barred from all government jobs as well as the fields of journalism and the arts. Jewish doctors could serve only Jewish patients.
- ❖ Jews were ordered to report to the local police and have their identity papers stamped with a "J."

---

[4] The tradition of erecting a Christmas tree for the Republic was an expression of nationalism and statehood. It was also used for causes such as donation drives and started by the man Olga references Rudolf *Těsnohlídek*, a Brno journalist and writer.

- ❖ Jewish children were expelled from all Czech schools.
- ❖ Jews were allowed to shop only during designated hours.
- ❖ Jews were forbidden to leave Prague or move without permission.
- ❖ Jews were barred from certain areas of the city, including the banks of the Vltava River.
- ❖ Dawn to dusk curfews; radios, snow skis, and driver's licenses were confiscated.
- ❖ Jews were barred from buses and trolleys.

An avalanche of decrees took away their rights and dignity. Could my father actually have formed a realistic picture of his parents' existence in the so-called Protectorate? In light of these relentless Nazi-imposed restrictions, it seemed surprising that my grandmother could devote any thought to the cost of Chinese pearls my father bought my mother for her engagement ring. Or that my grandfather could still revel in the beauty of Smetana's music. In their letters, Arnošt and Olga continued to express more significant concern for my father's circumstances than their own, as shown by Arnošt's response to the news that my parents were planning to leave China in early 1941:

> Overall, I think your plan to move to the USA and not continue traveling around China is the most reasonable one. We hope that you will finally find a permanent home there, and you will put a stop to this constant moving around that has really

hounded you ever since you were called up for the Army service.[5]

A week later, my grandmother wrote:

> Our postman has become so familiar with us that when he comes, he calls to Dad, "I don't have anything from Mr. Valdík" or, "a package of tea came again, coffee would be better," and so he entertains himself. However, I assure you that we need neither the first nor the latter. I stocked up in a time when everything was plentiful, and we are now slowly consuming it. So your shipments are only put on show in the glass cabinet for admiration by my acquaintances that see even through so much you haven't forgotten us.
>
> I kiss you and your Ruth Alice

This time, it was Arnošt who added an ominous postscript, informing Dad that he'd tried to send him his copy of Jaroslav Hašek's novel *The Good Soldier Švejk*:

> I just received word from the post office that it was confiscated.

The Nazis felt intimidated by the Czech farcical character, whose response as a bumbling soldier to the Austro-Hungarian Empire's irrational system was to outsmart the incompetence. Despite such occasional sour notes, the correspondence both ways continued to be regular and mostly cheerful as my parents moved on to California. The most significant difference was that my father's demanding new routine at the Long Beach hospital shifted much of

---

[5] Dad enlisted in the Army after graduating from Medical School in 1937 and escaped to China in Mid-1939.

the letter-writing responsibilities to Mom, who accepted the challenge with her usual charm and goodwill, as evidenced in this April 3, 1941, letter:

> Valdik is such a busy man these days that I am taking over the work of writing letters to our family. And I have wanted to write you one letter all of my own for a long time, so I thought I would sit down this afternoon and spend an hour or so with you.
>
> You would love to see Valdik rushing around and feeling so important. He carries around so much energy that it does my heart much good to see him really tired and ready to sleep at night. And I wish you could have seen him when he was looking for something to keep him busy when we first arrived in Los Angeles. I often thought of you and wished that you could have seen him. You can be so proud of him, Daddy and Mother Holzer.
>
> In less than two weeks, he had found this lovely place to live and work. I thought all along that I would have to take care of us both here for a while until Valdik had found something, but he was so fast that all I could get done was to watch him breathlessly! He is a good doctor. Kind and considerate and truly in love with his work, and the best is not too good for him. Maybe I am too partial—since I am his wife, but if I can think that, knowing him as well as I do, then surely it must be true!
>
> Don't you think so?

On June 8, 1941, Valdik's grandmother, Marie (née Porges) Holzer, wrote to him. As was typical for many older Czechs raised in the Austro-Hungarian Empire, Grandmother Marie wrote in an old German cursive handwriting known as *Kurrent* or *Kurrentschrift*.

> My dearest,
> May you always have luck, as you have, my dear Valdi, up to now. I was delighted by the last letter your dear father sent me

in which he told me that you are doing well in your job and that you already bought a car. Your dear Father wrote you about my illness. Thank God, I am already doing fine. With best wishes and be dearly kissed from your loving Grandmother.

Reading this short, simple letter brings a wave of tears to my eyes because I know what my father could not: it was the last letter he would ever receive from her.

As 1941 progressed, nothing remotely resembling normalcy was possible for Prague's Jews. Driver's licenses were confiscated in January. I can imagine what sad thoughts went through Arnošt's mind as he relinquished the license he had obtained twenty-seven years earlier, before the beginning of World War I. Soon after, Jews were prohibited from buying or even catching fish. In the winter, Jews were conscripted to shovel snow from the roads. They were forced to give up their apartments to Nazi officials in the nicer areas of Prague.

On August 2, 1941, my anxious dad commented in a letter to his cousin Hana Winternitz that this happened to Arnošt and Olga:

> The Germans are wreaking terrible havoc there, though our family has so far fared quite well if you can trust their reports. My parents were expelled from their apartment since the house was "Aryanized." They moved to Slezská Street on July 1. They didn't give me the address for whatever reason; every little stupidity now makes one worried.

Shopping was restricted to two hours in the afternoon; between 3:00-5:00 p.m. Jews were barred from attending movies, plays, concerts, and museums. They were forbidden to read newspapers (except for a Nazi-censored Jewish paper) or listen to the radio. They couldn't leave their homes after 8:00 p.m. I can be sure my father didn't realize the extent of these restrictions because a letter from Arnošt dated June 11, 1941, suggests that my dad had written to him about a movie he'd seen in America. I'm sure Dad wouldn't have done that if he'd known such mundane pleasures were forbidden to his loved ones.

> Your report about movie theaters is very nice. Unfortunately, we haven't known what a screen in a cinema looks like for a long time, let alone heard anything from a loudspeaker. All that we hear now is the gramophone, which we play daily in the evening after eight when we have to sit home nicely.

Yet even now, Arnošt brushed aside his son's offer to help them leave.

> As far as our quota is concerned, for now, we really do not pay attention to it. It will not be so soon anyway, and then Mom is very much afraid of seasickness. So we ask you, dear Valdi, though we know you are very kind and attentive and concerned about us, not to do or undertake anything until we ourselves call on you. We are pleased by your thoughtfulness, and it is a great solace for us that you care for us so much.

Decent, civilized people—my grandparents and so many others like them—caught in the Nazis' web could never have fathomed the regime's true nature. As much as I ached for Arnošt and Olga as I read these words, Arnošt's irrepressible sense of humor (so much like my father's) drew me out of despair and closer to him.

From July 12, 1941, this letter shows him in perfect form with reason to laugh at his latest misfortune in their newly settled apartment.

> And now I am copying a little article from the newspapers. It reads: "The long arm of the thief. On the balcony of his apartment in Slezská Street in Vinohrady, the owner of the apartment Arnošt Holzer, hung a short green man's fur coat with a possum lining to air it out. Not even in his wildest dreams would it have occurred to him that his little fur coat, which he thought safe on the balcony being aired out, would disappear completely. Nonetheless, that's what happened. Some scrounger with very long arms stealthily snatched the fur coat from the balcony. The owner suffered a loss, as he announced to the police where he went to complain and request that the detectives look for both the coat and the thief."
>
> As you see, our journalists have a sense of humor. The day of the event, I was cross at Mom for constantly cleaning and airing out clothes, but then I told myself, what's gone is gone, let's hope I am not going to Siberia. Here the frosts are not so bad, a good overcoat is good enough for me, and I have one, so let's have it; it was God's will. A lesson not to air out things on the balcony. You take care over there. They could filch something the same way there. Otherwise, no one in the family has lost anything, and everyone's health is holding, except for Uncle Gustav, who is, poor thing, at his last gasp. So generally, we can be content.

And at the end of the letter, a handwritten note from my grandmother displayed her sense of humor.

> You can imagine what has gone on with that fur coat. No one keeps airing things and cleaning so much as me, so Dad allegedly has long expected and known that something would surely get lost. He waited 32 years and was proved right.

This humor, warmth, and—most of all—love radiated from the letters of Arnošt and Olga throughout that summer. Despite this, I cried as I read them, knowing there was almost no chance for my grandparents to leave Prague by this time, and soon there would be none at all. I felt sure they must have sensed this but their messages, like their loving birthday greeting to my Dad, gave no hint of their suffering.

> Valdi, the next month you will celebrate your thirtieth birthday. This is a milestone in everyone's life. You will celebrate it away from us, so our thoughts will be with you. Were you with us, we would have tried our best to celebrate this day. Of course, Ruth will certainly remember the day nicely and will, at least in part, make up to you for what we cannot do for you.
>
> Unfortunately, a bad fate forces us to spend several years of your life without you. You know how we loved being with you and that we now must miss what was the most beautiful thing in our life and, in fact, for so long the purpose of our lives. Only the hope that the day will come when we can hug you again gives us the strength to bear all the hardship we must.

As their communication continued back and forth, I learned of my father's early love of cactus, an affection I observed in our well-drained sandy-soiled yard in Florida. After my dad had sent his parents photographs of Southern California cacti, Arnošt responded:

> We can see from them that you are content and how beautiful it must be there. Those cactuses have always been your hobbies, and Mom almost anxiously guards every specimen you once sent from Slovakia. When you are taking those to America one day, it will be quite a transportation challenge.

As I wondered about the apartment that the Nazis forced them to move into, a phrase gave me a painful glimpse of how claustrophobic my grandparents' lives had become. And yet, they never complained as their situation deteriorated.

> Dear Mom still and constantly worries about all those flowers. In our apartment, we don't have as much room as we used to, so she has to continually shift them, searching for a sunny spot so they would thrive.

Arnošt maintained his even, low-key tone in an August 10 reply to my father's repeated and now more urgent plea for his parents to come to America.

> Now the fall storms will start on the ocean—you know how Mom travels only with difficulty. And me, it would be a trip like the one I experienced with you, dear Valdi when we went from Venice to Trieste, and you wanted to disembark in the middle of the sea. Let's leave it till when the sea calms down, and there won't be such big waves on it.
>
> If you firmly decide to stay in the U.S. one day, then we are ready to follow you as soon as possible so we could live together with you. As we have written you a number of times, it wouldn't be a life for us only to longingly await a letter and a visit once every few years.

Just three weeks later, on September 1, Jews were ordered to wear the yellow Star of David pinned to the left front of their clothing. Arnošt tried to reassure his son.

> You must have read in your local newspaper about the strange symbol that we will wear on our chest in a week. We will soon know what general impression it will make. It is odd when we

read all the time how racially different we are, and because of this, we need to have that special badge so everyone can easily recognize us.

Although strange for Arnošt's cultured era, the use of badges and other articles of clothing as a way of identifying Jews was centuries old. In the early 1200s, the Catholic Church's Pope Innocent III had encouraged this. The earliest such symbol for Jewish men in the Czech lands was a yellow or white hat. Jewish women also were forced to wear a hair veil, usually a yellow band. In 1551, Ferdinand I initiated a new Jewish insignia—yellow circular badges worn on the left side of the breast, mandated for Jews over twelve. The distinctive markings exposed Jews to the danger of attack. The Jewish badge was abolished in 1781 by Austro-Hungarian Emperor Joseph II as part of a series of enlightened reforms throughout his lands.

Neither Arnošt nor my father could know the direct opposite of "enlightened reform" was about to begin on September 3 when the Germans inaugurated the first experimental gas chamber at Auschwitz using the insecticide Zyklon B to poison 850 prisoners. The Nazi nightmare escalated. My grandfather and father also had no idea that one year earlier, when Adolf Eichmann, one of the primary organizers of the "final solution to the Jewish question" arrived in Prague, he'd set into motion what he'd been carrying out in Vienna: the robbing and expulsion of Jews.

What Arnošt *did* know and dealt with was the extraordinary difficulty of maintaining any regular contact with my father. By September 1941, all Prague post offices were closed to Jews except for one on Ostrovní Street—one of the oldest, smallest, and least comfortable. It became the only place where around 56,000 people, a Jewish population swelled after Hitler conquered Austria and the Sudeten region, could mail letters. It was open only for two hours each afternoon, from 1:00-3:00 p.m. Phone calls weren't an option, and telegrams invited scrutiny, so mail was often the only way to communicate. When I think of today's world and the multitude of ways we communicate every day, I wonder if most of us can fathom what agony this would cause.

When Arnošt needed to send a letter, it would probably have taken him most of a day. Just getting there was difficult. Jews could only ride in the back of a tram's second car—if there were enough space available, and the crowds must have been enormous. The post office was about a forty-five-minute walk from their apartment at Slezská 125, but this also posed problems; by decree, Jews had to avoid walking on or across specific streets deemed too respectable for them to be seen.

Jews knew that even telling a joke about Hitler was a severe offense that might lead to imprisonment or death, so my grandparents' letters did not express any extreme viewpoints or disclose any critical details. The most revealing information was their list of rights lost through various Nazi proclamations as the months progressed. Arnošt couldn't even visit his ill mother in Benešov because travel was restricted. In late 1941, Jews were ordered to surrender their bicycles and typewriters, which explained why Arnošt took to writing his letters by hand. In December, all Jews had to turn over their sewing machines, cameras, ski gear, gramophones, and records. Over time, as more and more of the letters were translated, I began to understand Arnošt and Olga's use of code words, such as "spa" for a concentration camp. Mostly, I recognized their attempt to paint the illusion that "all is fine" for their adored son, just as my father did in his letters to them.

That fantasy became impossible to sustain on September 27, 1941, when Hitler placed his security boss, Reinhard Heydrich, in charge of the Protectorate. Another chief proponent of the "final solution" to rid the Nazi realm of Jews, Heydrich immediately launched a mass campaign of arrests and terror against all Czechs who showed the slightest resistance to German rule. On October 10, Heydrich gathered in Prague with Adolf Eichmann and other high-ranking officials to plan a ghetto in the eighteenth-century fortress town of Terezín, known in German as Theresienstadt. Built by Austrian Emperor Joseph II, the town was named after his mother, Empress Maria Theresa. The Nazis expelled all residents to create room for prisoners, but at first, the Czech citizenry had no way of knowing what was in store.

Within a short time, the transport of Czech Jews to Terezín began. Even Arnošt, the unflappable optimist, could not mistake what lay ahead as friends and neighbors began to disappear. He sent a cable to my father on October 22, 1941: "Go to the Travel Bureau Lubin Havana and get an entry visa and ship tickets for Ernst and Olga Holzer immediately."

Arnošt followed the cable with a letter that my father most likely received weeks later.

> Dear Children,
> We don't have any messages from you this week, so we have been without a letter for the last three weeks. Just now, we would need your words. In the previous letter, I told you that transports

are now being sent, but we still are calm and haven't asked you to undertake anything for us. Meanwhile, many of our acquaintances decided to send a cable to their relatives overseas to ask them for help in emigrating.

As you know, I have turned down your many offers to help. However, given the present circumstances that confront us and the advice of our many friends, and after much consideration, we decided to send you a telegraph. You surely received the cable, and we are waiting for your answer this week.

We don't want to burden you, and we hope that if you decide in our favor that your financial burden, however temporary, will be bearable for you. You will certainly also consider the obligations you took on for dear Ruth. We don't want your sacrifices to be at her expense.

We don't worry about making a living. In spite of my age, I feel strong enough to take any work. I don't have to write to you about your Mom's vitality. As you know, she overcame a hard time with her strong will, although she made the greatest sacrifices for us. We don't want to and will not owe you anything. We just need your immediate help so that we won't be sent away from here like I explained to you in detail last time.

Of our acquaintances, Dr. Langer and his wife and daughter have left on transports. Further registered for transports are the Steiners, also old Fischer, and perhaps also Lenda with family. That is all I wanted to write you about this matter.[6]

Yesterday Franta Schoenbaum and his boy visited us. He would like to leave now as well, but he faces obstacles that he won't be able to overcome easily. His boy is very nice. He is a rascal, so we had fun with him.

This time, I am not writing too much because I am really not in the mood for it these days. I hope that soon I will find my mental balance and find the resolve for a long letter.

---

[6] Lenda was Arnošt's brother, Leo Holzer; his family consisted of his wife Elsa and son Hanuš.

> With warm greetings and kisses,
> Your loving Father

There was also this from Olga:

> My Dear Valdik,
> You cannot even imagine how difficult it is to live here now. My wish was not to see anyone of my friends depart. The Langers already had my farewell; the Kes family is already waiting for a transport; Hanička [Steiner—a Valdik first cousin] and her husband will stay yet because pregnant women are not sent in transports. She is expecting little Růžička now in October. We now often regret that we did not travel to join you. I admit that we were afraid to burden you in a foreign country. We wish from the bottom of our hearts and souls to be united with you, but now, of course, we will have to leave it to fate whether it decides that we should see each other again.
> With kisses,
> Your Mom

How revealing... and heartbreaking! Through this short, simple note, I understood that my grandparents did indeed regret not leaving with my father in 1939 and that the reason they didn't do so was what I suspected: they honestly did not want to be a burden to him. I don't have to guess how my father reacted to his parents' sudden change of heart. Dad saved his correspondence with his first cousin once removed, Ferdinand "Uncle Bill" Breth, living in Pennsylvania, in which he asked for help rescuing his folks. His mother, Teresie, was the sister of dad's grandfather, Alois Holzer. Known as Uncle Bill to my dad, he'd made it to America well before WWII and worked for Sonneborn & Sons, headquartered in New York City, run by German-American Jews. Ferdinand was a Zionist.

When the first world war broke out, he volunteered for the Jewish Army in Palestine, serving as an officer in General Sir Edmund Allenby, the British General, that led the Egyptian Expeditionary Force to victory in Palestine and Syria.

By late 1941, it was nearly impossible to get a US visa. Arnošt's reference to Havana reflected the faint hope shared by many desperate European Jews that the island nation would be more welcoming. A handful of refugees had indeed managed to gain admission to Cuba, but corrupt consular officials who sold them phony visas victimized many more. The Cuban government turned others away even if they did hold valid papers. The most well-known example was the SS *St. Louis*, which sailed from Germany with more than 900 Jewish refugees in 1939. Only a few were allowed to disembark when the ship reached Cuba, and the United States refused to respond to passengers' pleas for asylum. The vast majority were forced to return to Europe and face the incipient Holocaust.

Dad knew that Uncle Bill had tried to help others with emigration problems. He hoped this kind man who had lent him sound advice, as well as $1,000 (2021 value: $13,600) upon arrival in the United States, might know how to cut swiftly through red tape. Bill's reply on October 29, 1941, offered little encouragement.

> Cables like the one you mentioned came probably by the hundreds. I received three, two from my sisters and one from Franz Holzer, who probably must be a cousin of ours as he was born in Jeníkov, whom I only met once in my life. They all ask the same thing—visas for Cuba.

Bill had generated a list of his closest relatives and narrowed it down to the twelve who most needed help.

> The travel agency told me that it is not difficult to get a visa, but the sum they quoted took my breath away. First of all, the Cuban Government demands a $2,000 deposit per person, which is supposed to be refunded when the immigrant leaves the country. However, a Cuban bank makes the deposit for you if you send them $150, which is, of course, not returned. Then next $250, the visas' cost; $500 sustenance deposit; and $250 for the return trip ticket—altogether $1,050 per person. To this may be added the cost of the steamship ticket from Lisbon to Havana, which is at present $510 per person. Multiply this by 12; you can visualize what I am up against and why I cannot help cousins like Franz.

The bottom money line was truly staggering, as was the cost of doing nothing toward rescuing the lives of these desperate people.

> If you want to rescue your parents, you will immediately need $2,100. {2021 value: $38,400} You can, of course, use the thousand dollars I lent you, and if you are absolutely unable to get the rest of the money, I will lend you some more, but please do not mention it when writing home because other relatives would swamp me with the same requests. It is hard to refuse. One feels like sentencing these people to deportation. God knows to where, yet my resources are limited. I am just a chemist, and all that I have was from saving from my salary. The issue is too big for one man to handle, yet it preys on my mind whenever I have to refuse.

The money from Uncle Bill's loan was undoubtedly no longer in Dad's wallet. Although he was now working, he had to pay rent along with other expenses of a married man, and he'd also bought a car. The average price of a new car in America in 1941 was $850 (2021: $15,125). Raising $2,100 to start a process that could ultimately cost much more must have seemed impossible. Now I understand why my usually sensible and skeptical father was taken in by Gaspar "Bilo" Mendez that November. Dad was becoming as desperate as his parents. Bilo, who worked as an orderly with Dad in the Long Beach Seaside Hospital, pretended to be well-positioned to get a visa for my grandparents. Bilo then swindled Dad out of the money he paid for the presumed visas by skipping town.

Amid all this came another letter from Arnošt and Olga dated November 22. In it, they were once again trying to allay my father's fears as they downplayed their concern.

> So far, five transports have left so, with them a few of my close acquaintances. Various messages have come from them, some of which calmed the nervous crowd. For the past three weeks, no transports have been sent. But there are rumors that they will be renewed at the end of this month. We are now very upset that we didn't consider the matter more carefully, given our impression of the first measures, and sent that telegram to you, Dr. Valdi. Today we would give much, much if we only could take it back. We could have avoided making your already hard position even harder and spared you all those sacrifices you had to make, the financial and physical ones, to obtain what we had asked you for so carelessly.
>
> Rules and regulations change very often here . . . now older people are forbidden to leave, so anything you might send wouldn't help. I beg of you not to incur any more unnecessary financial costs and not to take any further steps, and just to be satisfied with those you undertook already. You have done more than enough, and we hope that the time will come when we can return everything to you to the last coin.

> As soon as emigration from the country is opened again, we will let you know.

It was already too late. The only legal emigration from the Protectorate would have been on a Nazi transport. By autumn, the Nazis had stopped emigration out of German-controlled Europe. Terezín, thirty miles north of Prague, had originally been a resort reserved for Czech nobility. In the late eighteenth century, the walled fortress was named "Theresienstadt" in honor of the Austrian Empress Maria Theresa. Taken over by the Gestapo in 1940, we know now that the Nazis did not wait for Terezín to be ready before starting the evacuation of the Czech Jewish population. On October 16, 1941, the first transport was dispatched to Lodz, Poland, where the Germans had crowded many Jews into a ghetto. That transport was followed by four others during October, carrying 5,000 people. Among them was Milena Langer Ballenberger, wife of my father's close friend Bála and daughter of the lawyer "Dr. Langer" referred to in my grandfather's letters. Through documents, it was clear she and her two children were taken from Lodz to Auschwitz, where they were murdered, as were her parents.

The futility of escape may not have been apparent to my grandparents at this time, but it was becoming evident to Uncle Bill, as he revealed in a letter to my father dated December 5, 1941.

> In the Czech Colony in New York, there is a rumor that nobody is allowed to leave for America and that the Nazis never intended to release our relatives, and the only reason why they made them send the cables was to make us waste our money. Thus we cannot do anything but wait and hope for the best.

Within days, on December 7, 1941, the Japanese attacked Pearl Harbor, and while my parents listened to radio reports, the world was about to change forever. Germany declared war on the United States. No longer neutral, America was brought into the European conflict. That meant Arnošt and Olga were now behind enemy lines, making direct communication impossible. My father had nothing to sustain him now except blind hope, and even that nearly vanished with Uncle Bill's following letter, dated January 23.

> I do not know whether you have received any news from Bohemia, but I am afraid that everything we did for our people there was fruitless. I am now of the opinion that the cables which our relatives have sent us were inspired by the Nazis, who want to put the American Jews to considerable expense, the Nazis not having the slightest inclination to release their victims.

The only lifeline remaining to my father was the Red Cross's International Committee, which started a message service for civilians cut off by the war. Each note was limited to twenty-five words, about the length of a single tweet on Twitter. The forms were relayed via neutral Geneva but often passed through German censors' hands. The process was slow but popular, as it was the only means of contact for so many people. By the war's end, the Red Cross had relayed thirty million messages. Three from Arnošt and Olga were in my father's cache. The first was dated February 24, 1942:

> We are healthy and confirm your letter of November 23, 1941. With the best wishes to Chick's birthday and . . . to you from Mother!

While all the previous letters were signed "Táta" for "Dad," this was marked with his full name, with "Arnošt" Germanized to "Ernst Holzer." By this time, my parents had left California to visit my mother's family before continuing to Washington, DC. The message from Prague hadn't reached them when Arnošt wrote again, on March 13:

> Dear children! We hope that you are healthy, which we can also convey from our side. Hopefully, we will soon get good news from you. Our most sincere greetings and kisses, Ernst Holzer

Then, on March 26, 1942:

> We have already been without your news for a very long time and hope that all our messages have reached you. Otherwise, everything is the same.
> Wholeheartedly greeting and kissing you, Ernst Holzer

The message originated from the German Red Cross, was sent to the International Red Cross, and then passed to the American Red Cross. It bounced from my father's last known address in California to New York and finally to Indiana, postmarked October 18, 1943. My dad finally received it a year and a half after it was written. When I saw the last postmark on the envelope, my heart split open. My dad received it after the murder of his parents. It must have given him false hope that they were alive.

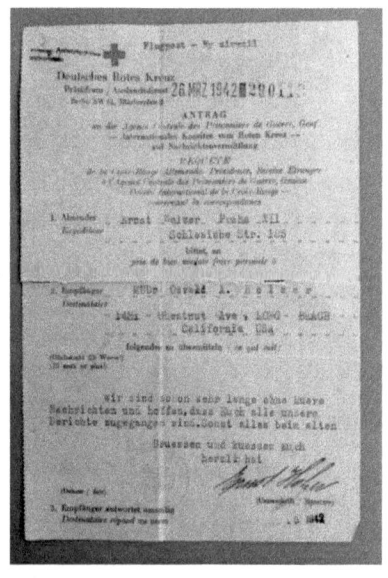

Arnošt (German: Ernst) Holzer, via German Red Cross

While it was impossible to send direct correspondence from wartime German territory to the United States except through the Red Cross, it was possible through neutral countries. Argentina maintained wartime relations with the United States out of a pragmatic desire to preserve trade relationships, despite ideological sympathy for the Nazis. On March 3, 1942, Arnošt and Olga sent a letter to Greta Steiner, a cousin who had immigrated to Argentina. Misplaced by the Steiners, my grandparents' correspondence finally reached my father in 1968. It arrived inside another letter from Greta, who had settled in Buenos Aires.

> Today we were rummaging through old letters, and among them, we found this letter, which we enclose. We think it will greatly interest you since it is the last letter by your parents addressed to us and comes from the year 1942. Since then, we did not have your address; we put it away and are only now sending it to you.

Written six weeks before the Nazis transported Olga and Arnošt to Terezín, the very faded envelope had undergone Nazi screening. It was covered with stickers and stamps: "*Examiner 6112*," "*Geöffnet,*" a swastika, and

Nazi Censor Marks

"*OPENED BY.*" The inner envelope was marked with Arnošt's return address and a 1942 postmark. How painful it must have been for my father to receive this in 1968, the next-to-last letter written to him by his father.

Inside the envelope was a fragile, significantly censored letter. Parts were entirely eradicated by black ink, likely when the message left Prague. It also appeared as if the censor might have used a match to burn away some of their words. The paper was brittle, and I struggled not to destroy it by unfolding it. Arnošt's beautiful cursive handwriting filled the top of the sheet, and Olga's followed. I thought of my father deciphering the precious remaining words. Arnošt wrote:

> As we have already written to you, we couldn't use your offer regarding the visa, since now any departure is impossible, even disregarding the war circumstances which don't make the ocean route any safer. Thank you again for your relentless offers. We only are awfully sorry that you had so much trouble with the effort and expenditures, all of it in vain. We must only hope now that the war fury will come to meet its end, and then we will be able to consider where and when we will reunite. Táta

Olga wrote:

> With day after day passing and no letter, only endless longing remains in the heart. We immensely miss your heart-filled letters; they always used to cheer up our lives. In my mind, I am kissing you and Ruth.
> Your loving Mom

In 1968 I was 325 miles away from home, attending Florida State University in Tallahassee. My father never told me that he received this heartbreaking missive. I unearthed it in 2008. I wished I had been there, sitting at Dad's side as he read, just as my son, Derick, had been at my side to help read his great grandfather's last letter to my father. I could have reassured my dad that he'd done the very best he could to save his parents and that an irrational force, not him, was to blame for their deaths. But what could I say to him about how the inescapable pain of the past had shaded his days? About how my father's unhealed memories could never permit him a homecoming without a different outcome?

My grandparents' letters were filled with tender phrases such as "with kisses" and "your always loving mom." I marveled at why a censor had blacked out descriptive parts of someone's eightieth birthday party and news of a wedding and a friend's baby. But even censored letters are better than none. Or are they? This painful letter tore open old wounds upon its arrival a quarter of a century after it was written. The note must have reminded Dad of his failed attempt to get a visa. In 1968, as he read his father's haunting words, Dad saw for sure his parents knew it was already too late to rescue them. But what (if any) peace could that bring to soothe survivor guilt?

I think my father held on to the letters when he was in China because they became—for him, a young man in a strange and foreign place far from friends and family—surrogates for the actual people he loved. If he had thrown them away, he would have had nothing to connect him to home. It was his lifeline to his lost past.

Preserving the letters accomplished something else. It meant their voices would be heard, lives remembered, and individuals memorialized through human stories in a manner that history books with all their facts sometimes fail to do because the emotions are washed away. By leaving the letters to find and decipher, my father defeated the censors and thwarted the Nazis. He shined a spotlight on the individuals and who they were or someday wanted to be. The letters provided their epitaph. As we read their words, we remember them. They are now a part of us.

Light Was Always There

"You know, when one gets out into the world, only then is one able to see what a conceited simpleton he has been. I realize more and more how unworldly and, in a way, provincial we are. And so, Adolf provided us with at least this profit, albeit we dearly paid for it."

VALDIK, written in Ping Ting, March 8, 1940,
to cousin Hana Winternitz in Great Britain

Valdik, 3 yrs. old—1914

Valdik, 17 yrs. old—1927

The gifts the letters bestowed upon me are many. As in an opening act, which sets up the rest of the play, I got to know my young father, which might be my favorite thing about the process. Several decades after the letters were written by Dad to his friends and relatives, I observed him leading a remarkably inspired life. He was extreme in both generosity and impatience, annoyed with those who wouldn't behave with honor. What happened to him was brutal, yet he never quit longing for fairness. He didn't allow misfortune to define him.

Thrust into an unfathomable universe, as with many forcibly displaced persons and refugees, my father exemplified the plight of an individual who adapts to the random absurdity of life without any particular knowledge of what may unfold next. After the loss of his native land and identity, he managed to create a new world in Florida, one in which he could survive and, on most occasions, thrive. I found myself wondering how and why this occurred.

My dad's own saved seventy carbon-copied letters illustrate how we humans can awaken and mature through the incidents and people we encounter in our lives. The correspondents' voices demonstrate how vital our role of self-determination is through the centrality of human choice and, thus, how the essence of our life evolves. We, and only we, decide our being. The power to choose to hope despite hopeless circumstances, pessimistic or optimistic, anguished or fulfilled, lies within each of us.

My father always lived his life as if he had just a few moments left. The thought that these secrets from his young adulthood were hiding in plain sight still amazes me. The demons he carried; doubts about how he could have, should have, tried harder. His suspicions that he ought to have known and done more but let the moment slip away or worse yet made the wrong choice; the friends and relatives he tried to protect by telling them, "Don't come to China." *What if?* I know he must have thought endlessly about it after settling in sun-filled Florida over a decade after living as an adventurer against his will.

Life is a series of choices: each option's consequences are uncertain. Until they are not. Haunted by what my father did or didn't do, he had lived a double life. You can't un-ring a bell. Beyond our shared DNA, his past circumstances carried my present life within them. I had to retrieve the details of years known only to him from those Chinese boxes when the private treasures of a lost Czech world became mine. As I began to digest what my father was saying in his letters, my heart pounded as he became more real to me than I sometimes am to myself. The letters ceased being objects and became subjects, which allowed me to experience his reality as my own. As I dared to amplify my imagination about how I might have reacted to what he went through, I found the center of my soul yearning for peace and marveling at how he handled it all.

The biggest challenge of assembling my books was determining what to leave out. Each letter held an overabundance of fascinating thoughts from forgotten times and places I'd studied only briefly in high school history class. *The Munich Agreement. The German people's charismatic attraction to Hitler. Antisemitism. The mandatory Star of David badge. Swastikas. Gestapo. Brownshirts. Japanese invading China. Blitz German 'lightning attack' bombing against the United Kingdom. Pearl Harbor. Propaganda and censorship. The Atomic Bomb. The Holocaust.* When they became personal, they came alive. My father died without knowing how his story would end. He left that to me. It became my responsibility to tell the world what he couldn't.

Dad looks so young, virile, and dapper in the many photos posted in his blue leather "escape album" that it's tempting to think he was confident in his triumph of survival, but it wasn't always so. His bouts of insecurity and uncertainty about the future resound in his words. He wrote with a maturity of insight and realism that made me both profoundly proud and sad.

On December 17, 1939, he wrote from Shanghai to his first cousin Rudolf Fisher, who had escaped to France:

> Of course, I would like to know what has happened at home. All the correspondence arrives opened [by censors], and mother writes some things that cause me to fear she'll get locked up. Otherwise, lately, they did not write much. Their letters are full of optimism, which I do not believe. My father is working up until now. They write that they have enough food; who can believe that? I am concerned about them, especially after the last uprising; the news is that they are evacuating those who are not "dependable" to Poland.

Reading these lines, it's easy to assume my father suspected even more than he let on and that his idea of what might happen frightened him. His continuing efforts stymied to get his parents out of Europe. He was careful to shield his feelings from them, just as they shielded him from the truth about their predicament; everyone was trying to sound upbeat—it was an act of love, not deception.

When he wrote to his friends and cousins, my dad dropped that shield just often enough to make me worry that he'd fallen into a depression, and as I read the correspondence, his misery became mine. Painful as this was, it helped me understand why he didn't want to share these letters, why he chose not to bring them out and casually reminisce with his children. Who in his right mind would want to remember such a painful past?

Consider this confession to his friend Rudla Rebhun in February 1940. My dad was about to depart the American Brethren hospital that he'd joined in Ping Ting Hsien for his Chinese language immersion studies in Peking. He'd just arrived at the remote place in Shansi Province, after a tumultuous journey by train and donkey:

> Despite all this fun, my soul is torn and discontent. I miss something all the time; it's not too hard on my soul out here, but only God knows what I want. I don't know it myself. Like I said, getting married might be it; that way, I would have someone to grumble to. The way it is now, no one understands me.

I'm tempted to say that I understand him, but I can't be sure. I know that his letters helped me see that my father was more complicated and tormented, more layered by his World War II past than he ever let on. With great stoicism, he made sure during his life we three children never shared any of his pain and yet also did his best to ensure that we reaped the benefits of his awful life lessons.

The letters and my research have raised as many questions as they've answered. I've never found the answer to the fundamental issue: How and why could this happen? Maybe I'll never know, but I will keep asking, searching, studying, and then sharing what I learn about these lives changed by hatred, war, and the Holocaust. The lessons about our shared humanity are just as pertinent in our world today. If we care enough to act, we can change the future. If not, if, as the wise say, we don't learn our lessons, humankind, at its worst, will repeat the process. Over and over . . .

To understand my young father's choices and state of mind, it's vital to understand what was happening in Shansi Province and throughout China. Two years before his arrival, in 1937, local warlords' ancient pattern of control was disrupted by Japan's invasion of the Chinese mainland. To resist this incursion, the Chinese Nationalists loyal to Chiang Kai-shek and the Chinese Communists dedicated to Mao Zedong had joined forces, temporarily as it turned out. Even though the Japanese invaders were better armed, their strategic problem was China's sheer size in proportion to their limited numbers. This situation offset their military superiority, and the result was a near stalemate.

The Japanese generally held coastal areas, railroads, roads, and towns, while the Chinese controlled the vast inland and tended to dominate the countryside, from which they could launch their attacks. The United States supported the Chinese, who hoped to keep the Japanese off-balance until (or if) the United States entered the war and forced the Japanese to direct their energies away from China.

By the time my father arrived, Shansi Province was in its third year as a contested territory. The Ping Ting county seat was occupied by the Japanese, while the surrounding countryside was in the hands of Chinese Communists. The conflict between Communist forces and the Japanese invaders was not a matter of distant gunfire, heard in safety from within the hospital walls, but a practical concern because Chinese guerillas regularly sought treatment.

In 1940, the *Star of Cathay*, the Brethren newsletter—the same newsletter that welcomed my father to the hospital staff—listed eighteen inpatient admissions to Ping Ting the previous year for gunshot and explosive wounds.

My dad noted the Japanese came to the hospital after the 6 p.m. curfew to ensure no guerillas were getting treatment. They would then count the number of patients, and in the morning, a patrol would come in for another headcount, reasoning that if the evening and morning numbers were the same, no guerillas were admitted overnight.

My dad then explained, "We used to keep a bunch of Chinese farmers who were ready for discharge and let them go during the night, and then we would admit some of the peasants—who obviously were in the Chinese Communist army—if they needed any medical care. Our census at night matched the count in the morning and vice versa." Adding to his challenges at the time, he was also dealing with an epidemic of typhus or spotted fever.

I realized how painful this period of my father's life had been for him—leaving his family and friends and shipping out to a distant and, by European standards, primitive country, where he knew no one and didn't speak the language. So why would this young man leave behind the final vestige of the familiar, the Czech refugee circle in Shanghai, and self-exile from this diaspora to travel to the dangerous backcountry of northern China where an airfield had been built by Japanese invaders outside the town shortly before he arrived?

He relayed one reason to his friend Bála as he tried to make sense of his situation: "I somehow feel adventurous... but all that is really against my will." His adventurousness had arisen from "some emigrant psychopathy when one gives into all kinds of things." He cited fits of anger that led him to kick a rickshaw and regret it a minute later. Writing to Czech refugee friend Karel Schoenbaum, studying at the University of Oxford in England, he blamed a widespread emigrant psychosis for a malignant atmosphere in the Shanghai Czech community. He was sick of the backbiting among the Czech émigrés in Shanghai. "One would drown another in a spoonful of water," he wrote to Bála. To Karel Schoenbaum, he wrote:

> I was rebuked for all kinds of things, for having too many foreign friends, for the fact that my favorite book is {The Good Soldier} Švejk, for lukewarm patriotism, and who knows what else.

Another reason to take off for the backcountry was curiosity about China itself. He wrote to a medical colleague that he was looking for something "really Chinese." On that same day, he wrote Franta that the real China only starts beyond Peking.

> There, where you have to travel by train in the darkness at night so no one could see the train traveling, wherein every car there is a team of [Japanese] soldiers with a heavy machine gun . . .

The other primary reason was an economic necessity, as he described the dire Shanghai situation to Franta:

> . . . one doctor could almost care for another, so many of us were there, and I was such a young greenhorn.

Even in remote Shansi, a doctor position was better than being unemployed in a city—better than walking around Shanghai with one's hands in one's pockets.

His decision to practice medicine in the interior was also born of concern for the suffering of sick and impoverished peasants and "coolies," as unskilled laborers were called at the time (a label now considered derogative). He may have underestimated the seriousness of the medical challenges he would have to deal with in Shansi. Still, even as Dad eventually became pessimistic about the medical mission's effectiveness in Ping Ting, he remained a conscientious and dedicated doctor.

The remoteness of the place would have been rugged for anyone from Europe to conceive. While there were several towns within walking distance of Valdik's hometown of Benešov, there were only two towns on the seventy-two-mile north-south road that linked Ping Ting to Liao Hsien. He kidded Rudla Rebhun that there was no donkey big enough to take him around. With both the town and hospital compound surrounded by walls and the gates closing at 6 p.m., electricity only working at night, and a broken radio, my very social father endured profound isolation. He was a stranger in an alien land with little in common with the Christian missionaries or the Chinese peasants.

Rarely could my dad send or receive a telegram because of the expense and unavailability in remote areas. Even if he had resources and access to such services, he couldn't arrange a phone call to call his parents because the Nazis took away the home telephones of Jews. He must have lived in constant uncertainty and fear for those he'd left behind.

He wrote this to his Aunt Erna Mautner in Chicago on February 5, 1940:

> I was receiving news that wasn't that bad from home, but the last letter really disturbed me. The note was sent right before Christmas, and I am not sure if it wasn't partially affected by the Christmas mood. My parents wrote that the situation back home is getting worse and that they are preparing, in the last resort, to leave Bohemia by evacuating to Poland. They reported that they don't believe that it would soon be necessary, but they want to be ready. My parents are getting informed about local conditions and have many questions about different business opportunities. Naturally, I got myself working on it, and I'm finding information so we won't be surprised. Of course, in that case, I would have to say no to any American journey. But I am still hoping that my parents won't have to leave, it would be horrible. If they get here, I could take care of them, but it would be an awful life.

Two days later, to his friend Franta Schoenbaum, he revealed a different side of himself as he wrote about trying to adapt to his strange new circumstances by opening to new experiences and challenges while feeling out of control.

> I am now the head physician of a provincial hospital. On Sundays, I go to sing in a church. I am learning Chinese. I live such a strange existence, an adventurer against my will. Maybe it will seem humorous to you. It cracks me up a great deal, but sometimes this all makes me terribly unhappy. Where will this lead? What will, I am asking you, come out of this?

I appreciated better that his struggles in China were probably all the more overwhelming because he hadn't expected to be there at all, as he wrote to a friend back home:

> As you know, I left Prague in May and got to Marseille, where I boarded a ship for China. I totally did not intend to reach the destination; I wanted to stay somewhere along the journey.

Valdik—American Brethren Hospital, Ping Ting Hsien, Shansi Province, 1940

What started as a goal to satisfy the Nazi bureaucracy became the best and probably the only choice, and so he embraced it as well as he could. He was determined to carry on as normally as possible. Although nothing around him seemed familiar, he could evoke and recreate his home comforts in reading, writing, and art. His ability to view life positively through his talents allowed him to control his bitterness toward his circumstances.

On March 22, 1940, he wrote to Aunt Erna in Chicago again:

> I am not sure if you know that I used to draw caricatures and had published photographs in different magazines. I used to make extra money while studying at the university in Bohemia. Now I am getting back to it. I am trying to make contact with some international magazines to make some extra money. I remembered Chicago's "Svornost" (Concord), and since I don't have their direct address, I am enclosing some of my creations. If you

could, please forward it when you find the address.

Dad certainly needed a few extra dollars at that point, but I know he'd have carried on with his caricatures regardless of commercial interest. He'd shared that the sketches he drew of his college professors had been hung on Charles University's walls. Many years later, when I accompanied my father on his last trip to Prague in 1995, I was astounded to see that they were still on display there!

I'm thankful he also relished the challenge of learning a new language, one of many my father was to absorb on his journey. On February 7, 1940, he wrote to Dr. Veselý, his head physician in the Czechoslovak army:

> In Shanghai, I first wildly procrastinated and then studied English. And from one lady . . . also Russian, the two languages I can now more or less wield. Of course, these are in addition to Czech, German, French, and soon-to-be Chinese.

On March 8, 1940, he wrote to his cousin Hana Winternitz in Britain:

> I am pleased to hear that you are making such strides with English. I am afraid that we will not be able to communicate when we meet as you will be speaking "Oxford" English and speak something between Australian and San Francisco English. Otherwise, I am mastering it quite well, and sometimes I even think it would be a good native tongue for my future children.

However, through all this, it's clear that his anxiety continued to build as he heard more about the realities of Nazi-occupied Prague while experiencing his setbacks in China. This August 10, 1940, letter to a mystery (to me) woman addressed as "Madame" captures his dilemma best:

> In July, my parents are still in Prague; they were expelled from their apartment and given a flat in Slezská ulice. It consists of only one room so you can imagine how it impacts them. Even though I am constantly trying to get them here, I cannot obtain the permits from local offices, and my parents are in no rush either. My father allegedly still works, and if one is to believe all their news, they are not suffering from any wrongs.
>
> I myself am living an adventurous life against my will. It would actually be quite nice if I did not have great responsibility for home. I already had my medical practice in Shanghai, which barely supported me, but then I got the position of the head of a missionary hospital in Shansi. Materially it was better but extremely adventurous in the interior of China. Nonetheless, I accepted the position. After my arrival, the only American nurse died, and there was no one to interpret for me into Chinese. Therefore, I had to go to Peking to school to learn Chinese. After a four-month stay in the hospital here, I will most likely again journey back; the conditions here are very insecure. I myself don't mind, I will probably get a position in another hospital, but I feel already like a gypsy. Otherwise, I did not compromise on my standards and gained experience, so I regret nothing. I will probably get visas to the US in the near future and will go there unless something extraordinary happens in the meantime.

I was thankful to see he added a final prophetic sentence that let me know he hadn't given up hope:

> With that, my whole adventure will probably end, and I will once again live a decent life.

Of course, he did achieve that and so much more, a decent

existence that I was privileged to witness. The letters allowed me to glimpse my father at a point when that outcome seemed far from certain, and the details of his future were unknowable—pieces I cannot conceive of without including my mother, my siblings, and me. Yet he did have a life before us, and the biggest shock of all is that it included other women.

In this regard, as I read the letters, I felt like an inconvenient witness and worried about the various possible consequences of his choices as a young man seeking love. I certainly never thought my father was celibate, so I'm hardly surprised at his occasional references to a fling or two in his travels. But some details are just too much for a devoted daughter to read, as in this letter to his friend Rudla in Shanghai:

> I got acquainted with one miss; she is no young woman, but she looks quite pleasing. She is half Chinese and half Mexican from Jamaica. She has money that she does not know what to do with. When one thinks about it, she was really supporting me in Tientsin. She was driving me by car around to do shopping, she was feeding me ice cream, and in general, she wants me to open a practice in Tientsin in order to bring me a rich Chinese clientele. I think she may have been in love with me.

I may even know her name from another letter my dad wrote to Leo Lilling, as his "visiting" Tientsin address was c/o Miss May Phang, 129 Canton Road B.C. Whoever she was, I'm glad Dad added this last line:

> Although I appreciated her company, I wasn't in love.

Thank goodness! I might not be here otherwise. I am grateful for her friendship with him during a difficult time. What became apparent is that some aspects of life are accidental and coincidental, but most are influenced by choice.

Description after description of the people my dad met enthralled me, such as this example from an August 1940 letter to Karel Ballenberger:

> One gets to meet Czechs all over the world. I met one leftover of the Russian Legions in Shansi. He was functioning there in a Japanese uniform as a member of some Russian crack unit. Now he has been—for several weeks already—"permanently resting," courtesy of the impact of a Red hand-grenade.

I was continually drawn to Dad's interactions and storytelling, like this from June 1940 to famous Czech author Dr. Miloslav Fábera:

> Several miles from us is a new road being built under Japanese supervision. Since there is fighting going on in this region, the engineers have a team of Russian bodyguards for their protection.
>
> I was sitting in my hospital office about two in the afternoon reading some papers. Suddenly someone knocks, which is very unusual because the Chinese burst in without knocking. In the door appears a white man in khaki, and he isn't exactly clean and groomed. Once I already had such a character in the hospital, the secret that I can speak Russian gave way, so I immediately started talking.
>
> A youngster about twenty years old, blond fluff on his chin, he was clutching his cap in his hands. He wasn't rushing in from the door and was only smiling at me. He let me disgorge questions for a while and then says: "Hey, please, I not sick, but I was told there is a Czech doc here, so I came around to see ya."
> I stayed as stiff as after polio since that chap spoke Czech, but

this strange Czech with a touch of Russian. "My name is Vejvoda," he says. "My daddy left fifteen years ago for Prague. He wrote me once and then nothing. I wanted to ask you where I should write to reach him and how to talk to him." And so he was telling me all this and all his stories, and I could already see he was speaking in Russian a bit more like Czech. He is from Charbin (Harbin), and he is working as one of these bodyguards, but I was happy to have a chat in this mixture at least. Finally, he spat out that he does have a "pain," the one that's always talked about last. Syphilis.

The parade of beguiling characters my father met seems endless. As I read his letters, I felt connected to each of these people—yet Dad's descriptions weren't always enough to satisfy my curiosity. This interest in knowing more grew when my explorations brought me to my parents' artfully prepared wedding album. It was filled with message cards with printed names and handwritten notes from some of the people who attended their October 1940 wedding. I recognized the names Myers and Kohler. They were

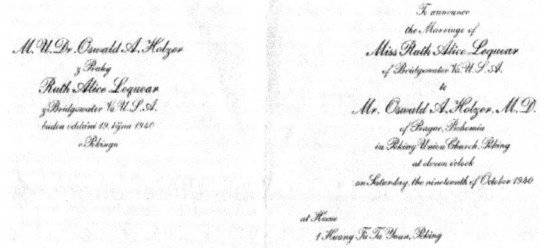
Wedding invitation

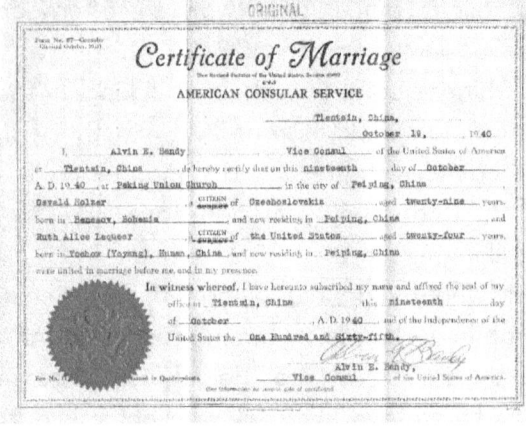
Wedding certificate

included in my mother's September 1940 letter to her parents when she informed them of her upcoming marriage to the young Czechoslovak refugee.

A few of the cards' wishes were indecipherable, written in German or Czech. Some hopes were expressed in English, such as "He who dares nothing, gains nothing—so go for it and God Bless," and "With the best wishes for a happy future!" They propelled me to wonder about these people who gathered for a wedding celebration following such a whirlwind courtship in this land of turmoil, and so I returned to my primary source: my dad's 1989 taped interviews.

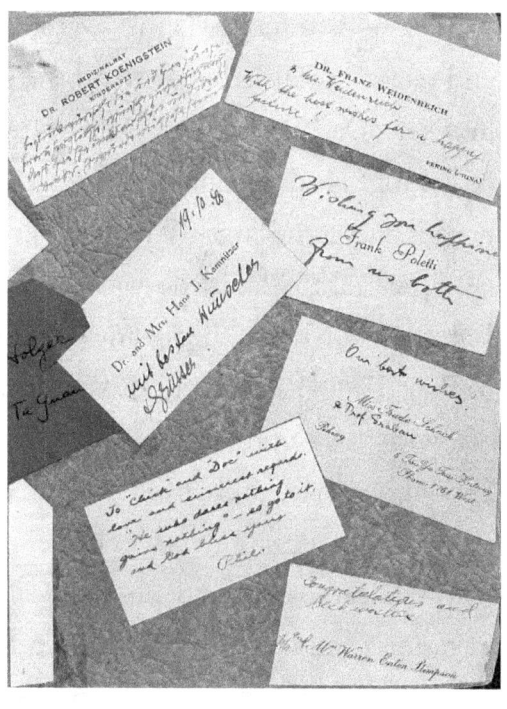

Wedding Album – congratulations cards

I found a few of the names included in stories from his two Peking sojourns. In early 1940, Dad had developed quite an impressive international social circle immediately after he'd arrived for his Chinese language immersion sponsored by the Brethren. With funding from the Rockefeller Foundation, the Peiping Union Medical College was at the heart of the intellectual ferment in Peking at the time. Dad achieved much social success in the expatriate community, centered on the Peking Club, a city within a city with a lovely clubhouse and tennis courts exclusively for foreigners. The expatriate community in Peking was congenial partly because instead of excluding my dad on account of his "curly hair," a nod to his Jewishness, it shut out "the degenerate Nazism and racism, totalitarianism, and the suppression of the free mind," he wrote. Dad worked hard at learning Chinese and also played hard in Peking. He'd become an official world citizen, invited to many parties and gatherings of the "foreigners."

Five months later, he was detained in Peking after a hospital shopping trip when the Japanese caused havoc along the route back to Ping Ting Hsien. Upon his return, he picked up where he'd left off with his sophisticated Peking social life and eventually, In September 1940, drew Mom into his fascinating circle. I could tell the wedding album messages came primarily from a mixture of her fellow missionaries and his medical, scientific, and International Legation friends. I furthered my search as I almost always did on my computer keyboard, asking Google's search engine for assistance.

From a 1984 *New York Times* obituary, I concluded that the cosmopolitan Mathias Komor, born in Hungary and with a doctorate from the University of Grenoble in France, became a well-known art dealer in New York City. He ran a gallery after settling in the United States in 1941. Komor and his wife likely left tumultuous China around the same time as my parents in early 1941. A leading authority on Chinese and related antiquities in New York City, Komor became one of the founders of the Asia Society, a member of the Metropolitan Museum of Art board, and a Fellow of the Japan Society.

A few more search engine clicks revealed that congratulations-card writer Dr. Franz Weidenreich was a German anatomist, paleoanthropologist, and renowned scholar. In 1935, Wiedenreich became honorary director of the Cenozoic Research Laboratory of China's Geological Survey. With his work on Peking Man's fossils and his observation of anatomical characteristics in common with modern Asians, he originated the "Weidenreich Theory of Human Evolution." This theory led to his polycentric evolution model of racial origins.

Another person who played prominently in my father's Peking intellectual life was a man named Amadeus William Grabau. Dr. Grabau was a former Columbia University professor in New York City. He'd left Columbia in 1919 after he separated from his wife because of pro-German attitudes during WWI. He was appointed professor at Peking National University with a specialty in geology and paleontology. Missionaries and scholars sustained the institution, and professors from England, Germany, and the United States made it a modern school of higher education. Professor Grabau undertook what subsequently made him famous, a geologic survey of China that gained him the name "the father of Chinese geology." Upon meeting my father, Grabau made it a point to invite him to his house parties, where an eclectic, intellectual crowd of foreigners regularly gathered.

Another fascinating character, often at the Sunday teas my father and mother attended at Professor Grabau's home, was Pierre Teilhard de Chardin—the French philosopher and Jesuit priest. He also was trained as a paleontologist and geologist. My mother was quite taken by Teilhard's spiritual reflections. Among my parents' belongings was a wedding present from their missionary friend,

W.B. Prentice. He gave them three books by Teilhard. Designated "for private circulation," Teilhard wrote them while in Peking: *How I Believe* (1936), *The Spirit of the Earth* (1936), and *A Personalistic Universe* (1937).

When I searched a website related to Teilhard's works, I came across a familiar name that was a part of Dad's social circle: Miss Fernande Saizeau. The mysterious Miss Saizeau corresponded with my father when her birthplace, Paris, fell to the Nazis. Their brief, heartfelt exchange was a favorite of mine. The website revealed that she was "a French artist and antique dealer." I wanted to know more.

In the Holzer collection, I found a small brochure from 1935 titled *Peking on Parade*. The inside cover advertisement provided me a little more information: "Asiatic Arts, Antiques . . . pottery, porcelain, paintings, lacquer furniture, rugs, etc. Semi-precious stones, Jades. F. Saizeau, 14 a Wu Lao Hutong (Soochow Hutong) F. Saizeau, Teleph. 1105 East."

There was no photo of the gallery owner. Still, a picture of two miniature bronze horses immediately made me recall the small, greenish-bronze Chinese deer dating from the fourth century BC that I chose from my parents' belongings. When I saw the ad, I guessed how the ancient deer came into my father's hands in Peking. Through the website Ancestry.com, a passenger manifest document showed that Miss Saizeau, age forty-one, entered America at San Francisco in May 1941. She undoubtedly had joined the mass exodus of "foreigners" who were encouraged to leave China around the same time my parents left. Sadly, Dr. Grabau was interned by the Japanese army in 1943 in a vacated British embassy in the Legation quarter. His health deteriorated while there, and he died shortly after being released in 1945.

Dad briefly spoke on the tapes about one man who particularly captured my imagination. Ignatius Timothy Trebitsch-Lincoln was a Hungarian-Jewish opportunist whose changing roles and identities made my head spin. At one time or another, he was an Anglican priest, a Protestant missionary, a British Member of Parliament, a German right-wing politician (and possible Japanese spy), and a Buddhist monk in China. Frequently transferring his allegiances, ultimately, he was recognized as a notorious imposter. At some point, he made it as far as Lhasa and translated the Bible into Tibetan. In the early 1930s, one of the Buddhist nuns where he resided was found dead under some peculiar circumstances, which pointed to Trebitsch-Lincoln as the guilty offender. He disappeared again and turned up in Shanghai, where he continued as a Buddhist monk.

Dad said that when the war started in Europe, Trebitsch-Lincoln sent a telegram to Hitler, Mussolini, and Churchill and the French government telling them that unless they stop the foolishness, the great father in Lhasa will bring a horrible disaster upon the whole earth. They wouldn't listen to him, and apparently, the great father in Lhasa didn't do anything either. Dad said the con artist subsequently became cozy with the Japanese.

He crossed my father's path in a coffee shop in Shanghai, introduced by friend Rudla Rebhun. Trebitsch-Lincoln's name appeared in a letter to my dad's good friend Franta Schoenbaum in Prague, written February 7, 1940, from Ping Ting Hsien:

> I will write a similar book of novellas like the one you are writing for amusement. I even wrote several stories already, naturally

> with illustrations; how else? The first story about a "farting missionary" is about a Grandpa who welcomed me in civilization's last promontory. Then I will write a story about Trebitsch Lincoln, who issues warnings to warring powers and corresponds with the Dalai Lama, who is now eight months old.

From the characters I met who wafted in and out of my dad's life, it became apparent why, in a March 3, 1940, letter to friend Karel Ballenberger in London, he felt compelled to describe what lay ahead for his book:

> The stories of good soldier Švejk will surely get some competition in my biography, which I intend to write and which I, upon the advice of Franta Schoenbaum, will call "In the Ass."

I chose not to use that title in the book I wrote of his life, *My Dear Boy*.

Dad closed by sliding into a sentimental tone in that same letter.

> And when you don't have anything to do again, write to me a long letter, larded with a political overview of the London Olympus and don't forget your friend who is again soon leaving for places that had previously been visited only by Sven Hedin and the missionaries. For that, I promise that next time I will for sure ride down the Wörlichsgraben together with you, on any snow and in any weather.

Here, Dad compared himself to a European explorer: Sven Hedin was a Swedish explorer and geographer who visited Asia. His reference to snow-skiing made me think again of *The Good Soldier* along with the Czech spirit of eternal optimism, seeing the future good during a bad situation.

As I got to know my young father through his letters, I realized the humor I learned from my youth had preceded me, but he displayed it only when he deemed appropriate. His tone, serious when writing to a former Czechoslovak Army officer or famous Czech author, would then turn bawdy with his male friends. In June 1940, he wrote to Franta Schoenbaum in Prague:

> As far as dirty talk is concerned, I managed to teach our doorman to greet me with "Kiss my ass," our missionary Ford is now called "Fart-Fart," and the smallest of boys at the mission can now say shit and ass, also backward. So I am now really starting to feel like I am among my own.

I also appreciated observing my father's growing maturity as he sized up the world he observed. This China prophecy captured my eye in a letter he wrote to Czech author Dr. Miloslav Fábera in Prague in June 1940:

> I, for myself, know that China is a land of opportunity at the time the Chinese-Japanese conflict will be ended. Then, there will be great progress. The land is waiting for organized work. Every hand that will help build the new China will be welcomed, I hope. Then they will find many helpers through the immigrant's technical hands. Soon there will be substantial industry because the richness of the land is inexhaustibly rich. It needs only to be organized. I hope then that the cultured States will wonder what China is producing and China will export it to all the world markets and trade fairs, and the Far East will not be lost to their export market. You only have to acknowledge where you live, get in touch with your surroundings, and not omit being a part of the culture. You have to admit the Yellow Race is no second-class citizen. This is a great thesis about immigration to the Far East, a position that none of the writers have written about so far.

My father willfully envisioned China returning to a country of consequence and forecast his role in that future as a "helper"—a hoped-for position that never came to be.

In this book, I've moved thematically instead of chronologically. So by now, if you've read my mother's "meeting letter" in *My Dear Boy*, you know Dad's China journey brought him exactly where he needed to be. My mom's description of my dad after knowing him just a few days was on point. She immediately understood his personality through and through. The only line in the letter I couldn't later prove was a statement about my grandfather Arnošt:

> Mr. H. owns a chocolate factory that is not in operation right now, and what will happen, no one knows.

Knowing my mom loved chocolate and suspecting that my dad probably figured that out quickly when they met, I wonder whether he fudged a little on that one small family fact as a way of gaining her affection. The specialized chocolatier of the Benešov family grocery store of old was understood by my mother to be the owner of a chocolate factory. My father's charm was already beginning to spark an everlasting light in my mother's life.

The Reflection of the Viewer

In May 1939, leaving Europe as an adventurer against his will, Dad lost sight of the shore in Marseilles, France; he encountered the unexpected in an uncertain world. He soon embraced the unforeseen as a photograph shows him standing dressed in a sailor-like suit and cap behind a ship's wheel, smiling broadly. The picture provides a glimpse of how he viewed the possibilities that lay ahead.

In the foreign lands, Dad encountered he expressed his feelings through the images his camera captured. With all its light and dark shadows, my father loved humanity. That is what I confirmed in the collection of photographs he'd tucked away. I viewed his pictures of peaceful sunsets taken some seven decades earlier. It wasn't hard for me to imagine him walking toward that future serene horizon we'd one day share in Florida along the Indian River shore where fiddler crabs scattered en masse before our sandy toes. But from his viewpoint, at that moment, his destiny was unresolved.

While the months moved along, I watched as Dad not only maintained his composure and compassion for life but kept his camera rolling. As I reviewed the volumes of black-and-white

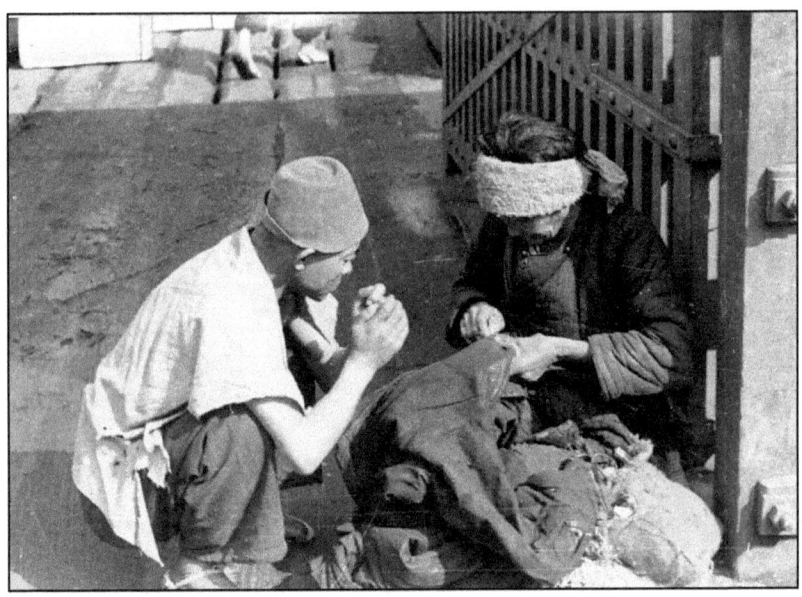

Street menders – Peking (Beijing), 1940

Man selling fruit, Peking (Beijing), 1940

photos and original Kodachrome slides that he left behind, along with 8- and 16-mm film, I was drawn into these exotic scenes just as he had been. I was amazed not by the striking landscapes but by the colorful humans who willingly and uncharacteristically let this stranger poke his lens into their midst. He often took portraits in the soft light of a shadow or, with his sharp eye, captured beautiful light, interesting textures of silk jackets, bold colors in brocade robes, or intimate close-ups. Many views were of the delicately carved elders' faces with lined expressions, seeking to share the stories told centuries before. No matter what they were doing as they met the small challenges of daily living—shaving heads, inhaling smoke from an opium pipe, pulling an overflowing oxen cart or empty rickshaw, riding a mangled camel or a braying donkey, preparing and selling food on a dusty street, washing clothes in a mud-filled lake—they continued with their activity as if to say, "Just watch me!"

After all that he'd left behind in Prague, photography helped my dad trust life a little more and found hope for the possibility of normalcy ahead. This acceptance of my father's invasive photography was unusual. At the time, in Chinese culture, a superstition prevailed—a belief that photographs can steal one's face. By their acquiescence letting my father photograph them, they profoundly shaped my understanding not only of their lives but of his. They showed me how he lived, whom he met, what made each day exciting. They gave me a gift I can never forget.

Many of the photos from the World War II period weren't in albums. They were loose, stuck in boxes, folders, or envelopes. Like a hunter on safari seeing everything as photographic prey, he captured people of all ages and places that he encountered. Most faces I can never match with an identification. I suspect he never heard the name of most of the Chinese people he photographed for a solid year and a half after he left Bohemia and then again during his service in 1946-47 for the United Nations Relief and Rehabilitation Administration (UNRRA). His connection with these strangers in their ancient villages and crowded cities was through his lens—visual, empathetic storytelling through intimate portraits of total strangers.

In the hospitals where he worked, he took photographs of the facilities and staff—but not of the patients, which he may have viewed as an invasion of privacy. With a dream to build a charity hospital somewhere in China revealed in a letter after he'd married my mother, I believe my father appreciated engagement in the patients' lives and wanted to use his skills to help them. I witnessed that patient connection in his later life. Dad grew to admire the Chinese people even though their customs and superstitions made him a little crazy. In the end, he sought to understand their culture, and they accepted him for who he was.

American Brethren Hospital, Ping Ting Hsien, Shansi Province, 1940

Seeing through my father's camera lens allowed me to share his wonder as he watched history unfold. I'm confident the most impressive sights of all for him were the vistas of America, land of the free, that he first viewed in mid-1942 with my mother as they sliced across the US's center to Washington, DC. Following a temporary rejection by the US Army for Dad to serve in the military, as he was technically still an officer and physician in the Czechoslovak Army (that no longer existed), they spent time living in snowy New York City before moving along to Lafayette, Indiana. While working at Home Hospital during this sojourn, my father received one of his most treasured lifetime honors—American citizenship through naturalization. Beyond achieving his goal of being a physician and raising and providing for his family, there was nothing that gave him more pride than being a citizen of the land of the free. He didn't have to worry about the Gestapo knocking on his door. He had freedom. "People die for it," he used to remind me.

Even after obtaining his American citizenship, my dad wasn't confident as a world citizen and adventurist where he belonged in the world. He and Mom seriously considered returning to China to open a charity hospital and school. Later, he contemplated returning to Czechoslovakia with his young family before the Communist takeover there in 1948. I saw in letters how seriously they considered returning together to their respective birthlands.

From a May 1946 letter written by my father's Aunt Valda:

> I read with much surprise your note that you plan to move to Czechoslovakia. I should be happy to have you here. I feel like your mother after our family shrunk so terribly, but I do not want to hide that I am afraid that you might encounter many inconveniences here in this post-war period. I presume that you live now in full happiness, and I should suffer if you do not feel comfortable here. On the other hand, our country misses

physicians here, and your profession thus gives much hope for the future. Keeping in mind your relationships and reputation in Prague's medical community, you would find a job immediately. But in fact, you have now already said that you plan to join UNRRA.

Reading the letters in chronological order allowed me to observe my father slowly accepting his situation, adapting to it, and then actually embracing his new life. This embrace was apparent when he finally met my mother, his nurturing anchor that moored him steadily with her love. Mom's letters, as well as his, allowed me to meet the man she fell madly in love with—her fun Czech lion. What she brought to him beyond the love was her passion for understanding. It became his tonic as she patiently continued throughout their lives to be his number one photo model on distant shores and close to home.

After some disappointment I encountered in the teenage years that led me to question my purpose, I remember Dad's counsel. It started with a Jewish proverb: "I ask not for a lighter burden, but for broader shoulders." It now holds more significance as he viewed suffering as optional. He continued: "The way I see it, life is meaningless. You must bring meaningfulness to it. That's what creates such an endless adventure, an opportunity to be more useful to those around you. My wish for you is that this life becomes all that you want it to be."

Wish granted.

The passion for photography that my father instilled in me has become one of my greatest joys. Beyond words are images. Each image is seen through eyes that observe things differently, via diverse experiences and influences that determine our viewpoint. Photography gives you a reason to travel and offers the unique opportunity to bring people together with no language barriers. From Dad, I learned the perfect shot could tell a story without a single word, and that editing sometimes removes that story farther from the authentic setting.

Valdik, Shansi Province, China 1940

Valdik taking Joanie's photo holding poodle, Pierre, 1957

What My Father Believed

"As you can see from my previous letters, I am slowly getting out of that émigré's hangover, and I am again starting to think straight. I believe that each of us has to overcome this initial after-surgery shock, like when one's tumor is cut out, one which deprives your organism of much energy. This was our unfailing trust in and love for a country that never really absorbed us fully, and even though we loved her and felt home within her, the others considered us strangers. You know, recently, I made up my mind about it all; I swept away my assimilationism and fought for new self-confidence. Maybe I am making a mistake, but it is my truth, one I am not scared to stare in the eyes of. I don't want to recall the old wrongs I felt from the moment when I began to meet with children at school. Even though I was raised in the spirit of the nation among whom I lived and of which I felt a part—there was not an occasion at which it wasn't made clear to me that I was an unwanted stranger. Whether it was at primary school, high school, at the University, in the army—everywhere I met with the sneer, though I tried to assimilate everything necessary . . . We shouldn't lie to ourselves. At least that's how I see it from the distance of one year, which I needed in order to digest it all. Now I am in a colored country. I became a member of a white community without the difference *of nationhood. I am considered on behalf of my personal qualities and not of my curly hair."*

VALDIK, written in Peking, April 18, 1940,
to Rudla Fischer in France

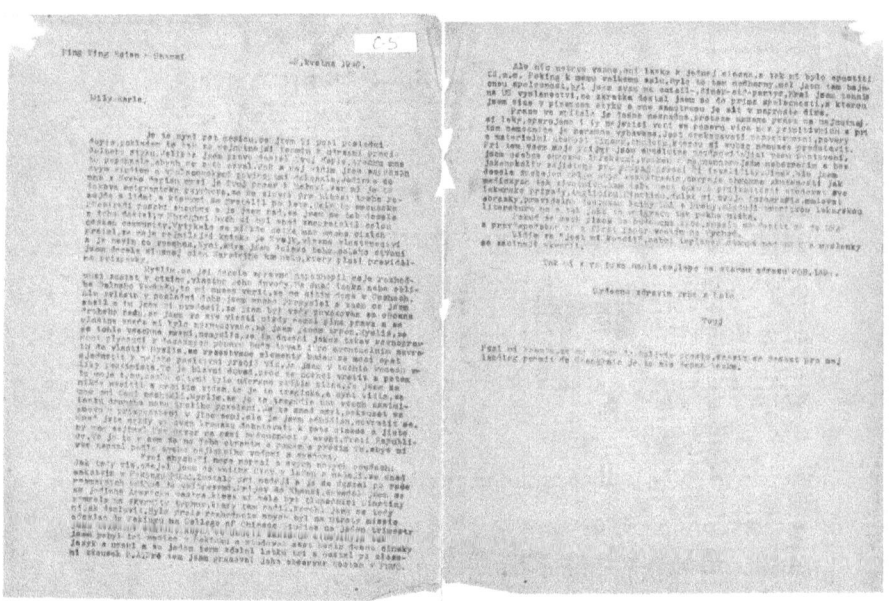

Valdik to Karel Schoenbaum (later Charles K. Sheldon), May 18, 1940
(C-5 letter, Holzer Collection)

"... *lately, especially lately, I have been thinking much about all that I have lived through. Then I came to a realization that I was always considered a citizen of a second degree, that I never had full rights in my homeland, and that really everywhere, it was implied to me that I was only being tolerated. Do you think that all this will change? Do you think that this present equality of sorts will last even after an eventual return to our homeland? Do you think that the various elements set against each other will again be able to unite towards some positive work? ... I believe that it is the tragedy of all of us assimilated ones, of the second and third*

generation. Possibly it is a mistake to try to adjust again to yet another country ... Maybe you discussed this issue in your [Masaryk] Club, and I would surely be most interested in your opinion about our future in the eventual Third Republic. This is where I am turning to you for help, and I beg you to write to me according to your best knowledge and conscience."
VALDIK, written in Ping Ting Hsien, May 18, 1940,
to Karel Schoenbaum in London

In the spring of 1940, my dad wrote these two remarkable, self-searching letters about his identity. What was he at his core, he wondered—a Czech, a Jew, or something else? I call them his "Testament Letters." They were the most difficult to read of all he had saved. He bravely acknowledged an inconvenient truth and was clearly in turmoil. Almost a year after arriving in China and one year before traveling to the United States, my dad began searching for respect, support, and compassion simply because he was human. I suspect his contemplative inner journey on this issue continued for his entire life.

As I was growing up, when asked whether a deity existed or not, my father professed to be agnostic. I naively accepted this statement of the unknowable from him without further analysis. I witnessed his many actions of great compassion for humanity and his strong character. "Is that not sufficient to make it to Heaven?" I would ask my young Presbyterian self. Five decades later, my discoveries in his letters help me better understand his complicated quest for his truth.

Through Ancestry.com, I found the ship's manifest on which my parents traveled to America in the spring of 1941. In a column under the heading "Race or People" by some ship official was scribbled passenger names identified as "English," "Russian," "American," or "Scandinavian."

Besides my mother's name was "American." Next to my father's name had been written "Slovak." It was crossed through by a customs officer and replaced with the word "Hebrew." Apparently, "Czech" or "Bohemian" was not an option for my curly-haired father.

The customs official was unaware of the life change my father had reached at the end of 1940. It was a monumental and mysterious decision that I didn't learn about until 2008. While going through my parents' effects, I spotted my father's name on a Peking "Certificate of Baptism and Confirmation."

> Osvald A. Holzer, son of Ernest Holzer and his wife Olga Holzer, born on the twenty-third day of July 1911 at Benešov, Bohemia. Christian Baptism and confirmation by me in the name of the Father and the Son and of the Holy Spirit on the twentieth day of November 1940, Rev. Edward T. Plitt Pastor, Evangelical and Reformed Church at Peiping {Beijing}, China

When I spotted the baptismal certificate with its image of Christ, it reminded me of a small cross I'd found among coins in Dad's leather change holder after he died. For as long as I could remember, this worn horseshoe-style leather pouch was where he carried his change along with his fingernail clipper. My brother found an exact replica of the cross in my mother's jewelry box. Puzzling. Seeing the baptismal certification led me to speculate that Reverend Plitt in Peking, who married my parents, gave them the crosses.

Osvald Holzer Certificate of Baptism

Was my father's baptism my mother's idea? Perhaps, but it's hard to know. Although she was a missionary, she never pushed Christianity on anyone. Everything she underlined in red in her Bible was about caring for and treating people, not how to browbeat or threaten them to her way of thinking. She freely shared her beliefs, and she probably worried back then about what ultimately happens to those who didn't accept Jesus Christ as their Savior. But Mom always placed confidence in everyone's freedom to decide how to lead their lives. Most important to my mom was that people abide by the Golden Rule—*Do unto others as you would have others do unto you*—an ethical concept shared by all religions. I am pretty confident Mom never insisted that my father convert as a marriage condition.

I can only speculate that my dad's struggle with ongoing worldwide anti-Semitism and his personal experiences with groundless disrespect may have left him open to exploring another future. A more practical possibility maybe that upon falling madly in love with my Christian missionary mother, my father decided on baptism as a way to please her and her missionary parents before he headed to America for a new chance at life.

Or could it have been that Mr. Arthur Ringwalt with the U. S. State Department, who'd arrived in Peking in December 1938 as Third Secretary, urged him to acquire a baptism certificate to present to anti-Semitic bureaucrats as he traveled to the United States? Ringwalt, who'd become a friend of my father during their tumultuous days in the Peking, knew there was widespread anti-Semitism in the US Congress and the Armed Forces, and even in his own State Department.

Fear of Axis spies entering the United States led to a reduced number of visas issued in 1940, and consul generals were instructed to prohibit entry to those deemed politically unreliable. Congress's visa policies had blocked actions to ease immigration which would have opened the country as a refuge for the Jews threatened by Hitler. The State Department supported Britain's policy, which tightened refugee allotments to Palestine. My father managed to get his paperwork just in time. In June 1941, the State Department forbade granting a visa to anyone who had relatives in the Axis-occupied territory.

I am sure I will never know what led to the baptismal certificate issued one month after my parents were married. For some questions, there are no answers. Perhaps Dad hinted at it when he smiled at me and repeated an old proverb: "Where two Jews, three opinions." I know that on some special occasions, he accompanied my mother to our Presbyterian Church. In his old age, when his weary heart warned him he was in the evening of his life, he attended a synagogue on Holocaust remembrance days. That's what his Jewish neighbors and close friends, the Cormans, told me after his death. The Cormans had accompanied my parents on a trip to Prague. They all visited the Jewish Quarter and the Pinkas Memorial that bears the names of our family members and theirs—all of whom were transported and perished in death camps.

My father never kept his Jewish heritage a secret. All three of us children asked him about his religious status at one time or another. To me, his answer never wavered: he stated he could not resolve what kind of God would allow the atrocities of World War II to occur. Nobody can choose what haunts them. At an early age, I learned that doubt (or denial of doubt) is an element of all religions.

The deadly threat to my father and the whole world came from people who lacked or ignored their doubt. They judged everyone, and the result was unfathomable suffering. After everything I had studied about the Nazi horrors, the devastating consequences of such blind judgment were driven home for me on a visit to the Holocaust Memorial Resource and Education Center of Florida. There I came across a poster entitled "Nuremberg Racial Laws, 1935." It included this description:

> *Translation of a chart distributed by the Nazi regime to inform the public of the complicated racial and legal distinctions between "full Jews" and first- and second-class "mixed breeds" (Mischlinge), enacted in 1935 as*

part of what was known as the Nuremberg racial laws.

Although I was familiar with the Nuremberg Laws, I hadn't studied their direct relevance to me. The 1935 law and subsequent attached regulations were the Nazi attempt to define a "Jew." I fell into the category of people with two Jewish grandparents, without Jewish religious affiliations, and not married to a Jew. Officially I'd have been declared an inferior citizen without full rights. With my "mixed" blood, I would have been a first-degree Mischlinge (*"Mischlinge ersten Grades"*) and would have lived in constant fear.

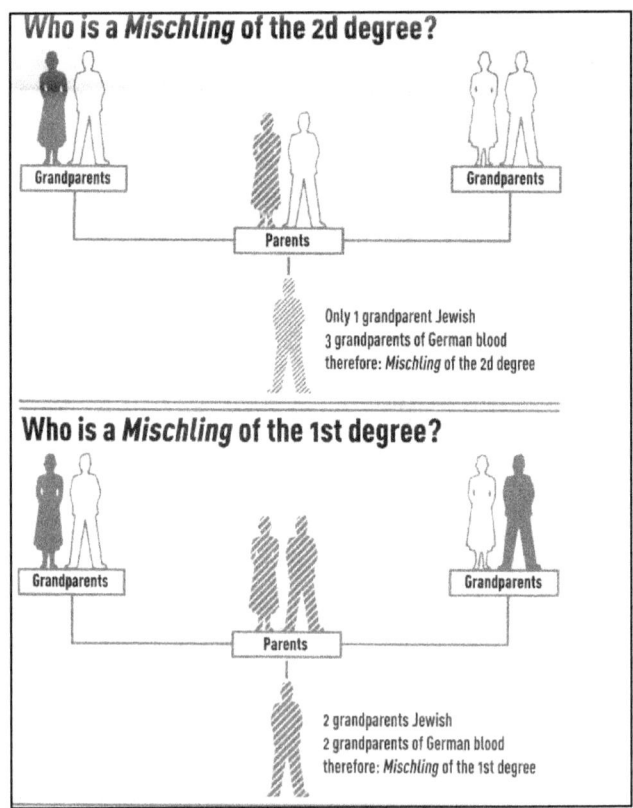

Nuremberg Law, 1935, "Mischlinge"

Late in the war, when Mischlinges (sometimes termed "mutts") became targets for deportation—for me, this would have occurred when I turned fourteen—had I been there, I would have looked at all the people around me who weren't Jewish and wondered who might choose to report me to the authorities.

And if I were lucky and nobody reported me to the Nazis—so many letter writers called my father "the lucky one"—I could have escaped to survive and rebuild my life. I would never have felt lucky. After all, I would have lost all that was dear to me: family, friends, and any treasured personal possessions. Seventy years after the Nuremberg Laws, I realized that regardless of whether I identified myself as a Jew or belonged to the Jewish religious community, I would not have been welcome in that purportedly civilized society, and my situation extremely precarious. In modern times, if some fanatic group is so inclined to differentiate us, they will use DNA tests to find what heritage they'd like to punish.

Another piece of information that my father's longtime office nurse, Sue Barge, shared with me gave me relevant insight I had been missing in my search to understand my dad's spiritual side. I am forever grateful to her. Sue told me about a time in my father's office when she, a Baptist, had a rare discussion about religion with my dad. He said there was only one religion he would consider joining—the Baha'i faith. Sue could not recollect anything more about the conversation.

Bewildered and having no knowledge of Baha'i and my father's interest in the subject, I searched the Internet. On the official site www.bahai.org was the answer to how my dad viewed God's will:

The Faith's Founder was Baha'ullah, a Persian nobleman from Tehran who, in the mid-nineteenth century, left a life of princely comfort and security and, in the face of intense persecution and deprivation, brought to humanity a stirring new message of peace and unity. Bahá'u'lláh claimed to be a new and independent Messenger from God. His work and influence parallel that of Abraham, Krishna, Moses, Zoroaster, Buddha, Christ, and Muhammad. Baha'is view Bahá'u'lláh as the most recent in this succession of divine Messengers.

The essential message of Bahá'u'lláh is that of unity. To bring a peaceful, global civilization, there should be an abandonment of all prejudice and a commonwealth of nations where scientific knowledge and reason are in harmony with religion. He taught that there is only one God, that there is only one human race, and that all the world's religions represent stages in the revelation of God's will and purpose for humanity. In this day, Bahá'u'lláh said, humanity has collectively come of age. As foretold in all of the world's scriptures, the time has arrived for the uniting of all peoples into a peaceful and integrated global society. "The earth is but one country and mankind its citizens," he wrote.[7]

As I marveled at the words on the screen, I realized I had known one of these citizens of the prophet's wished-for united earth with its peaceful and integrated global society. From the ashes of evil, sparked by my grandfather's letter, I witnessed my father come of age and carry on a meaningful life with my mother's unwavering love and support. And who on this earth has the right to judge my father's spiritual path? I never met anyone more compassionate

---

[7] http://gy.bahai.org/intro.html

toward others. He was a model for caring and truth, which I believe should be the cornerstone of all faith and every religion's foundation. And for those who choose to think we have one life to live here on earth, and that's all there is, no God to meet us in an afterlife, they too can serve as a model for caring and truth.

What does it mean to accept one's suffering? What does it mean to have faith? What causes humans to wage genocide? Who *really* knows? Why does someone teach their children to hate? These are all questions I've pondered. Now I better understand the choice my father made. He had lived between fear and hope and grew to believe we should not just tolerate another but exist equally with respect. My dad led a life that the higher being I choose to follow would admire—one like my mother's higher being— filled with love and peace. Dad gave meaning to all our lives with his love and respect for the world's people, and through his compassionate service, he brought overall purpose to human existence.

A benefactor to the suffering humanity . . .

Dealing With the Circumstance

In an early August 1940 letter to his friend Karel Schoenbaum, my father wrote that *the love of one young woman would never last.* Dad was wrong. He would not have flourished in the second half of his life had he not met my mother one month after he'd made that proclamation. They lived long and happily, their love strengthened by adversity as they overcame obstacles from the moment of their union. By reading his letters leading up to their marriage, I know he was ready for her benevolence and beauty to enter his life.

Without her support, I don't know how he could have dealt with the pain and guilt he carried throughout his days. The best clue to how stubbornly he struggled with the overwhelming truth of his family's murder—and the murder of millions more—emerged from a conversation recorded by my second cousin Tom Weiss one year before my dad's death.

Tom (Fischer) Weiss, 2012

"My parents, my uncles, my aunts, the

whole bunch died at Auschwitz," Dad said. "I don't discuss it—I don't think it is anybody's business."

Long silence.

"Yep. How much those people suffered."

Tom noted that his family had faced the same fate. Tom's grandmother Karolina, my father's Aunt Babi, who perished at Treblinka death camp, owned a Prague perfume shop. She was forced to turn it over to the Nazis, who gave it to a German watchmaker after looting. Tom's maternal grandfather was a prosperous businessman in Vienna. His entire enterprise was "Aryanized." Read: *stolen*.

"You know, it is strange," Dad replied. "They say we are lucky. We are the lucky survivors."

Tom (Fischer) Weiss & Father Rudolf Fischer, 1938

Dad expressed his own way of making sense of the incomprehensible; the Nazis were common thugs to him. "The whole thing was simple. It was a robbery," he said. "They just wanted to take what those people had."

"Yes, but with a certain amount of ethnic hatred too," Tom replied,

Dad didn't change course. As a man of tolerance and inclusion, he didn't want to acknowledge what evil lay at the center of the Nazi heart. Their desire to rid the world of whoever they labeled "degenerate" remained a concept my father couldn't or wouldn't deal with.

"They stole their houses, belongings, furnishings, carpets, everything," he said, adding sarcastically, "They gave it to the poor suffering Germans." He sighed, and then entirely in character as the Dad I remembered, signaled the end of all such talk by asking, "Are you hungry?"

The recording reminded me that my father died without knowing the truth of where his parents perished—he'd assumed Auschwitz, but it was more likely Sobibor. Not that it mattered where; what mattered is that the Nazis murdered them. Nothing can change that ending.

The conversation between Tom and my dad made me think of the debate that continues among thoughtful people who seek to understand what went wrong with the hearts and minds of so many to allow these war crimes—or any war crimes—to occur. The web of complicity in the Holocaust was far-reaching. If humanity wants to end genocide, we must continue to contemplate the history of the Holocaust and try to understand why it happened. We must also study what has led to other genocides since the Holocaust.

Many Germans and non-Germans were involved in the so-called Final Solution and the broader Holocaust atrocities that slaughtered millions of people and not just Jews. Some five million Roma Gypsies, people with physical and mental disabilities, homosexuals, dissenting clergy, Socialists, Communists, and other political enemies, people having a different philosophy or appearance all perished. Governments worldwide did little to confront Hitler's anti-Semitic ranting, raving, and death threats that he followed before everyone's eyes. These governments made it nearly impossible for the vulnerable to escape Hitler and the Nazis—they enacted restrictive immigration policies and onerous documentation requirements. Religious institutions and courts were complicit. To this day, stores in Berlin and Prague still sell confiscated silver. Museums worldwide harbor the confiscated artwork of owners who can no longer ask for the return of their possessions. Almost a century after the fact, we haven't entirely figured out how to right these many wrongs and change hateful attitudes when they flame up. Countless good people continue to seek justice and a true path to worldwide human rights protection. As I witness the many faces of new refugees, with so many displaced children, I wonder if we will ever achieve what songwriter John Lennon imagined as the time when "the world will live as one."

Aunt Valda Marik with son Jiri, 1927

Thuggery and thievery were not limited to the Germans. For my father, a December 1945 letter from Aunt Valda was emblematic of a widespread problem during those times. Writing from her family's Neveklov homestead seven months after the war ended for Czechoslovakia, she began cordially, commenting on my eighteen-month-old brother Tom and her then twenty-two-year-old son, Jiří. He spent much of the war in German forced labor camps, as did his non-Jewish father, Jaroslav.

> This week we received your nice letter for which we thank you for the nice picture of little Tomík. He must be very cute, and I am only sorry that I cannot see him for real. Jiří took photos of your dear wife and Tom to Prague so he could boast about them to his friends.

Aunt Valda then wrote of confronting realities:

Aunt Valda Marik 1945 letter

> For a long time, I was hoping and always waiting for some of our loved ones to return. I still cannot reconcile with the terrible fate they left, never to return. You can't even imagine, dear Valdi, how difficult it is for me to bear. I never imagined that something like that would even be possible.

Aunt Valda updated my father on the theft of his parents' belongings, which they had left with the janitor's daughter of their Prague Slezská apartment building.

> And now I have to write to you about the situation with that Miss Nenadalová, with whom your parents deposited a great many things for safekeeping. As I think I have already written to you, your dad left the list with us in a sealed envelope with the wish that we open it only if he wouldn't return. And therein it was written where he deposited what items . . . Nenadalová first admitted to having the things, but when Jiří went there twice to

take some of the items with him, she excused herself. She did not give him anything. Then, her lawyer wrote to me that I am not eligible to ask for the things because she agreed with Mr. Holzer that she would only return them to him. I got so angry.

The list included four Persian rugs, three etchings by Max Švabinský, several Rosenthal figures and porcelain cups, one bronze figure by Julius Lankáš, Meissen plates and figures, one bronze chandelier, and one porcelain dining set for twelve people. It described clothing like one gentleman's brown suit, one gentleman's dark gray suit, one ladies' coat with fur, and far more.

The belongings no doubt meant a lot to my grandparents. Their intrinsic meaning likely exceeded monetary value. Švabinský is a famous Czech painter of portraits and social scenes. He was proclaimed "National Artist" after the war. Meissen and Rosenthal are renowned makers of porcelain. Lankáš—my father's close friend and fellow patron of the Mánes Café—became a well-known sculptor.

Aunt Valda closed her letter with:

> It would be good if you, dear Valdi, give me discretional powers in writing so I would have something in hand. I will try to save whatever can be saved, but I don't have high hopes. Unfortunately, it is all the same in many cases. It is almost unbelievable how bad people can be and how they try to gain from other people's misfortune.

In a string of follow-up letters, Aunt Valda reminded my dad she was still looking for his power of attorney so she could pursue the issue. She grew frustrated with him for not responding to her request. His wound was fresh; "things" would not return his missing parents. The Nazis had stolen what mattered most—his nuclear family, his homeland. No power could bring them back.

It was not the first time Czech culture had been in mortal danger. Wars of religion, invasion, and occupation filled its turbulent history, but these cruelties could not compare. Six decades later, as I sifted through the accounts of what happened to my father's homeland after he escaped, a grim picture emerged of what Dad held within his broken heart. So much destruction: universities and schools closed; students imprisoned, tortured, and murdered; professors incarcerated and their scientific collections destroyed; literary and scientific libraries closed; homes confiscated; the works of the greatest Czech poets and novelists forbidden by censorship and confiscated; art was stolen; monuments demolished. This undertaking involved an insidious, well-thought-out plan executed at the highest levels of the Nazi hierarchy.

My parents became an army of two in our peaceful seaside community, looking for ways to create a better place, living not with indifference but by making a difference. They chose to do more than care. They put actions to work. I feel blessed that this was their choice. My mom kept Dad focused on his virtuous character and intent. "You don't have to be your circumstance" was one of her favorite phrases.

Dad's longtime nurse, Sue, made it clear my mother's patience was an essential part of Dad's success. Sue told me that my father was the best intuitive diagnostician she had ever served. She confirmed how patients loved to hear his exciting stories, that he was generous and forward-thinking in providing medical care. Smiling, she recalled a day when my parents were headed to

Orlando to catch a flight to vacation in some foreign country. My mother arrived in her car to pick my father up from the office. Earlier in the day, a patient had dropped off thank-you flowers for some treatment my dad had provided gratis. My father insisted they bring the bouquet with them. My mother repeated a few times it made no sense as they were getting on a plane in two hours, but my father could be stubborn. Taking the colorful flowers from the vase, he handed them to my mother. She and Sue exchanged sympathetic glances, and without another word, my mom gently carried the dripping bouquet out to the car.

Mom's generosity of spirit was also critical to my father and a quality he shared. One of the best examples of his forgiving nature turned up in the paperwork I uncovered related to Dad's dealings with Gaspar Mendez. He was the shyster in Long Beach, California, who'd failed to deliver on his promise to help my grandparents emigrate to the United States in 1941. Years later, my parents were living on Long Island, New York, when a letter dated January 17, 1948, arrived from Justin Bennett of the US Department of Justice, Immigration and Naturalization Service:

> It has been ascertained from the files of the Long Beach Police Department that in January 1942, you filed a complaint with the Bunco Detail against one Gasper Bilo Mendez, a Panamanian, who was then employed as a janitor at the Seaside Memorial Hospital, alleging that he had swindled you out of the sum of $300 in October 1941 in connection with a proposed plan to effect the removal of your parents from Czechoslovakia to Chile through the assistance of an alleged personal friend of Mendez then in the Chilean consular or diplomatic service.
>
> Through roundabout inquiry, your wife's uncle, Henry

> Kroeger, was contacted by mail, and your address was obtained from him.
>
> Mendez, who has been found an unlawful resident of the United States and subject to expulsion, has applied for suspension of deportation on the basis of having a United States citizen wife and two U.S.-born children. In connection with such application he is required to establish that he has been a person of good moral character for the past five years. If he knowingly and willfully defrauded you, this office would like to have the particulars, which you might specify in an affidavit executed before a Notary Public . . ."

Seven years had passed since my father had fallen for the false promises of Bilo Mendez. Six years had elapsed since the murder of his parents at the hands of the Nazis. In a typed draft of a saved letter written to Mr. Bennett in January 1942, I could see both my father's and mother's hands and hearts at work as they recounted what had transpired in the fraud.

In a world that had denied my father and his family justice during World War II, the concluding paragraph was admirable without malice.

> Though it is not my wish to harm the apparently innocent family involved by the witness that I have recorded for you, I hope that it may assist you in your efforts to deal with the case justly.

To this day, I do not know the resolution in the Bilo Mendez case. Perhaps it doesn't matter. In relying on him, my father made a poor choice for a good reason. It's likely at that point, he had no choice at all. It is clear from my dad's account and from the opinion of other voices he preserved within his letters, there's a certain amount of luck that makes all our lives go one way or another.

When my father concluded his 1999 interview with cousin Tom Weiss, he shed more light on the importance of considering how difficult that time had been. "I am sorry for your father's misbehavior—if there was any misbehavior," he said, referring to Tom's dad, Rudla Fischer, in mid-1940, inexplicably deserting his refugee wife and son in France and going to Great Britain. Torn apart and placed in great danger, the family never reconciled. "You know, during the war, these situations happened all of a sudden. Whether you acted right or not right, hard to tell, you had to make a decision—'I will leave; I will be back tomorrow.' There was no tomorrow."

Dad was silent for a moment and then continued. "It's like what I could have done with Hana Steiner, a first cousin that I could have married before I left Prague to protect her. She could have gone to China with me as my wife, and then when we arrived in Shanghai, I could have divorced her, no problem. It didn't happen. I did not know they would kill the whole family."

In the end, my father made many unimaginable choices. Decisions where mistakes meant other people died. After the war, the choices needed to address a new challenge—how to move on. I see the message as pertinent to our lives today. The choice that matters is how we deal with the outcome, whether we overcome or succumb to the situation.

Do we dwell on what can go wrong or think of all that can go right? In the end, my father and my mother chose to seek out the goodness in the world. They had the future—there *was* a tomorrow. What might have happened or not happened would never be known. *You don't have to be your circumstance.*

Going Home

Holzer Home and Store, Benešov, drawing 1904
(from Jewish Cemetery memorial)

Benešov Tennis Club, circa 1918, Valdik front row, left

"Hopefully, education and knowledge of history linked together with pure compassion and humanity will let us recognize the origins of old-new dangers and tie down the demons of hatred and evil before they grow to overcome us again."

VÁCLAV HAVEL, first president of the Czech Republic[8]

At my parents' memorial service, we played a recording of "Goin' Home," a song based on the famous *Largo* from Czech composer Antonín Dvořák's *Symphony No. 9*. Mom and Dad had separately chosen this song for their eventual memorials, knowing it

---

[8] From a speech given at the opening of the conference "The Holocaust Phenomenon" in Rudolf´s Gallery of Prague Castle, October 6, 1999.

was a song of hope that death is not the end.

For my father, 'going home' also had a more literal meaning. With guarded contemplation, Dad was determined not to be a stranger who'd lost his way back. His postwar trips to Czechoslovakia were always emotional reunions with the land of his birth, none more so than his first return in 1963 when he experienced what life under Communism meant for his freedom-loving compatriots. Afterward, upon his return to the United States, he wrote a letter to fellow Benešovian Dr. Ella Baumgartlova-Traub, a longtime friend living in New York City:

> The trip to Prague was a true revelation. Although they don't suffer any material shortages and can purchase just about anything they want if they have the money, the tension and lack of personal liberty are striking. I was treated royally by everybody. Although people don't like to meet in public places because of fear of being spied on, they talk quite freely at home. Some of our old friends are good Communists, but when you get to their homes, they open up. Vláďa Wagner just got out of jail, where he spent one and half years for telling some silly joke about the government. He was denounced in court by another friend of ours, Vláďa Padonec.
>
> Professor Šula told me that life under the Nazis was more tolerable because at least you knew who your enemy was, but today it may be your best friend who is spying on you.
>
> I have to confess that I bawled more in the five days in Prague than I did the rest of my life. To see the beautiful city so dirty and neglected—the people like characters in the "Actors & Beggars" opera; was sometimes hard to take. Benešov is something that one cannot describe. There is no plaster on many houses—the naked bricks are showing—nothing has been painted for the last thirty years. There has been all kinds of sloppy building going on that doesn't look good. I have the privilege of being the landlord

of the Chairman of the local Communist cell. He is living in our apartment. Our house and the property outside of town were not nationalized since they belong to a foreign citizen—that is me.

Dad returned to Czechoslovakia ten more times. He knew there was no love so sweet as to be among his kindred souls and old friends who survived. While his homeland was still behind the Soviet Union's Iron Curtain, my brother and sister individually accompanied Dad on separate trips. In 1995, along with my husband Roger and son Derick, I had the privilege of traveling there with Dad once, meeting some of his old friends and our Czech cousins, hearing them say "Welcome back home!" and visiting Dad's old haunts. He walked us through Mánes Café overlooking the Vltava River with a great view of Prague National Theatre, only mentioning he'd been there long ago. Combining old with new unfolding before my eyes, I stopped for a photograph of the white functionalist building housing the café and exhibition hall with the Vltava River floating underneath and a fifteenth-century water tower rising above. The letters I later read and my subsequent interviews with his friends revealed the importance of that place to his youth. I yearn for one more opportunity to hear tales of Café Mánes and Dad's artist allies in the gallery.

My father's death in 2000 was not the end of my emotional attachment to the Czech lands. My journey through history revealed by the letters gave me fresh reasons to return. I continue digging for answers and each time see the landmarks and faces in a new light.

Roger and I returned to the Czech Republic in 2009, 2011, 2014, and 2018. The 2014 trip coincided with the publication of *Adventurers*

Against Their Will in the Czech language—a high point in my writing journey. The trip was an emotional roller coaster. Twenty years had passed since the Czech people emerged safely from behind the Iron Curtain. No longer caught between dark chapters of oppression since the Velvet Revolution, they had restored their cherished freedom. At our Prague arrival, I was whisked off by a public relations consultant for an interview with the host of one of the most-watched Czech television talk shows. The show was hyped under the header: "The lost history of Czech Jews in exile has finally emerged from the coffin." I'd never done simultaneous translation, with a translator in an earplug immediately reacting to what the host said and then my response. The show went well, and afterward, the charming young male host rushed up to me to share quietly that his grandmother was Jewish, and he related to my stories through things she had told him. Early the following day, we spent time with Aunt Valda's grandson, my second cousin Tomáš Mařík, who mapped out our plans for the month-long visit to ensure time was spent productively. The first days of our pilgrimage in this city of spires included a visit to the Charles University Archive, where we uncovered many of my father's medical school records.

The documents revealed two Prague addresses where he had lived with his parents in the early- to late-1930s, so we went to see them. The last building, Slezská 125, was where the Nazis forced my grandparents to move in 1941 along with other Jews whose apartments were confiscated. During our visit, shockingly, freshly painted on the exterior brick wall were large scrawled letters of *Jude*, the German word for Jew. This was the word that appeared on the required yellow star for their apparel during Nazi rule. It's very rare to see this defamation in modern Prague because of a now-tiny Jewish population. I took a photograph so I wouldn't forget the kind of nasty assault my grandparents faced as they tried to go about their daily lives under the Nazis.

With my primary translator, new friend, and award-winning filmmaker Lukáš Přibyl, Roger and I toured Terezín concentration camp, a town built for seven thousand where the Nazis forced sixty thousand to live behind a fortress wall. It was a hideous place. Disease had been rampant, and food and medicine scarce. We saw where my great-grandmother, Marie Holzer, lost her life to pneumonia in December 1942 and the ovens where she was cremated. We lit candles in remembrance of this gentle eighty-year-old woman who died there solely because she was Jewish. We walked to the nearby Ohře River, where the Nazis threw her ashes along with the remains of thousands of others in an attempt at war's end to hide the evidence of their atrocities.

At Terezín, where my grandparents spent a month before their Nazi transport to the east, we saw cramped, triple-deck beds in living quarters. We had initially thought we would travel to Sobibor on Poland's eastern border at the end of the trip and share the family reunion in Benešov mid-month. Because of conflicting schedules, we made the family reunion the last event of the journey on May 30. Therefore, we adjusted our five-day trip to include Sobibor, Auschwitz, and Majdanek, in addition to crucial personal sites in Slovakia and Bohemia that my father had mentioned in the 1989 taped interview.

The long journey to Sobibor was emotional. Cousin Tomáš Mařík took a week off from work to allow adequate time to visit significant places related to my research for my books. To get to Sobibor, Tomáš drove us in his green diesel-powered Peugeot through the Czech Republic, Slovakia, and Poland. On a crisp, chilly early morning, Tomáš began by taking us to my grandfather's ancestral Čechtice village. Traveling down a fruit-tree-lined country lane stopping at the family retreat at Růžkovy Lhotice, seventy kilometers southeast of Prague, we came upon the site of Holzer family reunions since the mid-1800s. We toured the Orlík Castle ruins in Humpolec, where my grandmother's relatives may have lived centuries earlier. In Brno, we saw the elegant railroad station, where my father boarded the train after escaping the Nazi-controlled Czechoslovak Army as he covertly made his way to Prague to reunite with his parents.

As we drove on modern highways, I saw traces of snow on the high Tatra Mountains, where my father skied while serving as the staff doctor in the Army Officer Mountain Corps. We visited Prešov and the railroad station where Czechoslovak Army troops had gathered after the March 1939 German occupation, unsure what to do next. In the middle of the night, with brave orders from above, they assembled their tanks and trucks onto a train, repositioning near Brno in Moravia, closer to Prague. From there, my father, wearing gray riding britches, wrote his own order to inspect the meat supply, placed official-looking stamps all over it, fooled the German guard at the gate, and with good fortune on his side, eventually earned his way home rather than facing a firing squad as a deserter.

After three days on the winding roads, we arrived in Lublin, Poland. Robert Kuwalek and Beata Siwek-Ciupak, Lublin District

Map showing Sobibor within Lublin, Poland district death camps (photo taken at Sobibor museum)

experts from the Majdanek Concentration Camp Memorial staff, recommended by the USHMM, joined us for the ninety-minute drive from Lublin to Sobibor.

On the day before I set foot on Sobibor's bloodstained soil, I realized how significant the changed date for our family reunion had become. In an odd twist of fate, the visit to Sobibor was *exactly* sixty-seventy years to the day that my grandparents arrived on Az Transport from Terezín as passengers 906 and 907. Even if fate played a part, I wasn't sure I was ready for our impending visit.

Located in a dense pine forest, five kilometers from the Ukraine border, the Nazis chose the 580-acre death camp precisely because of its isolation. As we drove nine kilometers from the nearest town, Wlodawa, we passed several small pastures for goats but very few houses. With a mixture of growing excitement and foreboding, I saw the railroad tracks running alongside the roadway that delivered my grandparents to their final destination. The sound of the transports moving along the tracks brought to life in Steven Spielberg's movie Schindler's List came alive in my head.

While my heart and head pounded, we arrived at a clearing in the woods. A train platform appeared and a red building, the Sobibor Museum, offered a small parking lot. A children's soccer goal stood eerily before us in a field. Robert explained how the green, two-story house with flower boxes that we were looking at had been confiscated in 1941 from the Polish Forestry Service for the Nazi commandant's house. I wondered what malicious soul had occupied the place—someone who knew exactly the extermination of humanity planned there. After the war, the house returned to the same forestry purpose, and it was no longer a part of Sobibor. Robert said it was a family home now with children—thus the soccer goal.

The beautiful blue-sky day was silent. The only unwelcome visitors outside the museum were large hairy-legged horseflies swarming from the nearby swamps that further isolated the killing grounds in the dark days of 1942. The insects reminded me of my youth on our island in Florida, half a globe away. At the entrance stood a five-foot stone wall with the name 'Sobibor' and eight bronze plaques representing countries whose people died in this hellhole. The wording reflected the victims' many languages: English, Yiddish, Hebrew, Polish, German, Dutch, French, and Czech.

All but the Russians had officially erected a memorial plaque. With long-held animosity for Poland, the Soviets (at the time of the commemoration) ignored the request to participate.

The inscription under the giant letters spelling Sobibor read:

> At this site, between the years 1942 and 1943, there existed a Nazi Death Camp where 250,000 Jews and approximately 1,000 Poles were murdered.

No more than fifty feet away, children played soccer. I watched for a moment before turning my attention back to a past that was now my own.

Under that inscription in smaller letters was the story for which Sobibor is remembered:

> On October 14, 1943, during the Armed Revolt by Jewish Prisoners, the Nazis were overpowered, and several hundred prisoners escaped to Freedom. Following this revolt, the death camp ceased to function.

We spent thirty minutes in the small memorial museum learning all we could of the history of Sobibor, a human extermination camp created by the disgusting mind of Reinhard Heydrich and his like-minded Nazi team. That same week we visited, there was extensive news about John Demjanjuk, a Ukrainian Sobibor guard (later a retired Ohio autoworker), who had escaped to the United States. As an older man who'd kept his youthful secret, Germany was now extraditing him for his long-ago deadly deeds.

In the museum, we saw his name on a list of guards. It was chilling "evidence" about this Nazi war criminal that hung unnoticed for many years on the cold wall along with other accompanists. Was he on duty in May 1942? Had he noticed Arnošt and Olga's faces as he herded them to the gas chambers? Or had he walked to the field where the firing squads stood by. Months later, when Demjanjuk's penalty came down for the mass murder of 28,060, his five-year sentence equated to ninety-three minutes per life lost at Sobibor.

Most killed at Sobibor were Polish, but there were also citizens of Holland, France, Germany, Austria, Ukraine, Belarus, and the modern-day Czech Republic and Slovakia. They were Jews, as well as other people Nazis deemed to be "undesirables." On the day of the revolt, a brave group of about 300 prisoners undertook an escape attempt. Because of barbwire fences, the swamp surrounding most of the camp, and the armed guards' shooting, only fifty-eight people survived. It was the largest mass breakout at any of the Nazi death camps during WWII.

The Nazis tried—afraid those survivors would tell their stories to the world—tried to hide the atrocities. They tore down the buildings involved in killing 250,000 people and planted rows of pine trees. Today that is what one encounters—tall trees, with roots that grew from the blood and ashes of the dead.

After seeing the museum, Roger, Tomáš, Robert, Beata, and I walked the sandy path my grandparents would have taken as victims of the earliest transports to Sobibor, down a road the Nazis named *Himmelstrasse*—Street

Robert Kuwalek and Joanie at Sobibor, May 27, 2009

Trees along the Nazi named: *Street to Heaven* (path to the gas chambers)

to Heaven or Heavenly Way. In 1942 this was surrounded by barbed wire. In 2009, we could still see traces in the pine trees from the wires' embrace. As my father would have done had he ever gotten to this desolate place, I took photographs of these reminders of Sobibor's dark past.

After my grandparents were transported to Sobibor, Robert said they were separated, forced to undress, and then either taken in a group to be shot or, more likely, put in a building subsequently filled with poison gas. At that early time in the operation of the death camp, their bodies were placed in mass graves. In 2009, we stood in silence, looking at the grass that had covered those graves.

Next to the field was a large spherical memorial erected by a German nonprofit organization, a mound surrounded by a concrete wall filled with ashes and covered with small stones. During our time there, three other groups visited the memorial and walked down a path named The Avenue of Remembrance. Descendants of the victims have purchased plaques to honor their family members, each placed on large stones in front of a new pine tree planted this time with love, not hate, along the path.

Two hours after we arrived, we got in our car to leave. My voice cracked as I asked Robert how long my grandparents would have been there that fateful day. For a moment, Robert looked at me with tremendous empathy before responding, "They would only have been here about two hours before they were killed." It was the exact amount of time we had spent—two hours on the same day, sixty-seven years later.

And if that was not enough to form a major lump in my throat: we visited this horrendous site on May 27, the very day in 1942 its mastermind, Reinhard Heydrich, was attacked in Prague by assassins: soldiers of the Czechoslovak army-in-exile in Great Britain, aided by on-the-ground Czech resistance. During his role as Protectorate of Bohemia and Moravia under Hitler, his brutal nature earned him the nickname Butcher of Prague. For Hitler, Heydrich led the overall charge for the "Final Solution" to rid Europe of Jews, and Sobibor was a piece of that plan. Heydrich was well-prepared for vicious acts. He served Hitler in many sinister roles, including the right hand of the Reich SS leader, Heinrich Himmler.

Heydrich's assassination was perhaps the most important deed of the Czech resistance movement against the Nazi occupation. My Czech translators have cited speculation that had Heydrich lived, he would have been a likely candidate to replace Hitler if the need arose. Thus, on this exact day of history which was so significant for me and our world collectively, it eerily marked when a government-sponsored assassination of the highest-ranked Nazi officer took place.

As I stood on Sobibor soil, I felt an odd sense of accomplishment. I realized that when I am most weary and in need of strength, my grandfather's words sustain me. I started my discovery journey receiving the translation of my grandfather's final letter, written just three days before he began his train ride to eternity. His last wish delivered the compassionate spirit for how he lived and died from his soul to mine. His message to my father meant for us all. And, from the great beyond, I was invited to share it.

New Vines, Strong Roots

After we visited Sobibor, I was reminded of the miracle of it all at our family reunion. Eighteen Czech relatives, ages five months to eighty-five years, shared an incredible time, starting with a four-hour lunch at Benešov's *Restaurace U Zvonice* (in English "The Belfry," where bells are hung). Coordinated by Aunt Valda's youngest son, Pavel Mařík, and his kind-beyond-words nephew Tomáš, the day was a joyous family celebration. After arriving in my father's hometown Benešov, greeted by a town sign with the golden-yellow eight-pointed star of the original Sternberg noble family coat-of-arms, our festivities began with an unexpected musical performance in the town's small square. A small group of singers appeared to have materialized out of nowhere to provide a welcome home to our group. As we walked to the restaurant, my eyes filled with tears. I remembered from my interview with my dad how he described how his father loved to sing. I pictured Arnošt singing in his a cappella quartet under the watchful eyes of Olga and young Valdik.

Czech Family Reunion, Joanie with cousins Hanuš Holzer, 80, Tomas Mařík, 59, and Pavel Mařík, 80

I came prepared to the reunion with photographs of unidentified relatives ready to be recognized, digital copies for each family of the original Czech letters, a PowerPoint presentation showcasing the Holzer collection, and more. Tomáš and I secretly arranged for a joint birthday cake for the two cousins, Pavel Mařík and Hanuš Holzer, turning eighty years old within a month of each other.

The small restaurant was empty except for us. One twenty-foot table was set to accommodate us all; at first, only filled water glasses shared our table. I thought of the bond of blood we shared beyond water and wondered if the language barrier would stand in the way of connecting the branches of our shared roots.

Pavel, son of Valerie and Jaroslav Mařík (a mixed marriage-she Jewish, he Christian), Hanuš, son of Leo and Elsa Holzer (a Jewish marriage), and Věra Stehlík Lokvencová, age eighty-five, daughter of Miloslav and Božena Stehlík (a Protestant marriage) all came with stories of extraordinary lives. Pavel and Hanuš were ten years old when the war started, and Věra was just fifteen.

Vera and Pavel shared grandparents; their grandfather Frantisek Marik served as Benešov's Mayor at the Czechoslovak First Republic time after WWI. Her husband and brother were soldiers-officers in the army. The Nazis in 1942 locked up her father, Miloslav Stehlik, in various concentration camps, ending in Bautzen (Budyšín in Czech) in eastern Saxony, Germany, where he died. Vera's brother Mita Stehlik was my father's cousin and a good friend. Mita served in WWII as a colonel of the Czechoslovak army. In the Stalinist time (behind the "Iron Curtain") around 1960, he was sentenced to a long-lasting prison term around 1950, liberated after more than ten years when the Russians invaded Czechoslovakia in 1968. Mita emigrated to Canada, where he stayed the rest of his life. Vera and my warm connection was immediate. In a letter she sent me later with photographs and a drawing, I realized our admiration was mutual. At eighty-five years old, she wrote: "I hope fate will be with us, and soon we'll have another opportunity to embrace each other." With fate on our side, our embrace happened again in 2011.

When the occupation began, Pavel, considered a Jew by the Nazis, was forbidden an education at a critical time in his youth. His father, Jaroslav, was sent to a forced labor camp, as was his brother, Jiri, 23. His mother, Aunt Valda, was confined to a collection camp in Prague on Hagibor, getting ready to be transported to Terezín. A long story of intrigue allowed her to avoid the transport via a well-known dentist, Dr. Vanecek, who had her operated on, and the

Nazis lost track of her. Thirteen-year-old Pavel lived alone, working as an apprentice in a grocery store and dairy, not suspected as a Jew to the owner and his wife, who saw him only as a poor orphan. After the war, Pavel received a civil engineering degree from the Czech Technical University in Prague. Pavel became a well-known and respected expert in underground engineering, consulting on significant tunnel projects. Before he set out entirely on his career, in 1951, the communist regime concluded that he, a son of an "entrepreneur and enemy of the regime," had to enlist in the army and work in Ostrava mines. When his compulsory military service ended, he was hired by a company, working his way into the position of the director of civil works.

Later, Pavel worked for the PUDIS company, advancing to Department Director, despite being a non-Communist party man. His work included tunnels throughout the land. After Pavel founded his own private consulting business firm in 1993, forty-five years after the 1948 communist nationalization of his father's firm, Pavel worked on the detailed design for the Strahov tunnel. A major road tunnel, Strahov is considered the first and longest of its kind in the Czech Republic and an essential part of the Prague City circuit of transportation.

I was astonished to learn of Pavel's fame in an occupation similar to my brother Tom—his degrees in engineering geology and hydrology allowed him to lead a long and distinguished career with the United States Geological Survey (USGS). My over three-decade-long job in the geotechnical engineering consulting business world enhanced my respect and understanding for what Pavel and Tom accomplished in their careers.

Hanuš, whose youthful formal education was also stolen from him, received a life education from Terezín (Theresienstadt) that most people cannot fathom. Of almost 150,000 transported Jews who were held or passed through Terezín to the east's killing centers, roughly eighty percent died either in the ghetto or deported elsewhere. In the last days of the Terezín ghetto before liberation, Hanuš was one of 150 surviving children. His mother, Elsa, survived, but his father Leo Holzer, Arnošt's brother, died at Dachau in 1944, right before the war ended. Hanuš, who arrived at Terezín at ten years of age and left at fourteen, went on to become an industry and government consultant. In a twist of ironies, he created a prosperous existence for his family, living in Switzerland. As an advisor to the German Volkswagen's Chairman, Hanuš helped facilitate the Czech brand ŠKODA becoming a part of the Volkswagen Group in 1991—a story captured in Jan Králik's book: *The Man Between VW and Skoda—In the Background Hanuš Holzer.*

Věra became a homemaker, enduring the forty-year-long Communist era before finding freedom in 1989 in the new Republic. Pavel and Hanuš, with entirely different wartime survival experiences, agreed to be interviewed by documentary film producer Lukáš Přibyl so we could preserve their stories for all time.

In 1595, the town of Benešov gained brewing rights for beer. Later the brewery named a beer Ferdinand after its most famous resident, Austro-Hungarian's Crown Prince (Franz) František Ferdinand d'Este. Ferdinand's assassination in 1918 in Sarajevo is sometimes called the "spark" that lit a chain of events that led to World War I. Brewed of the best malts and hops the Bohemian Lands could give to the world, I knew my dad would have liked that Restaurace U

Zvonice served Ferdinand traditional beer at our reunion. After a light tap of our glass against another drink, we placed our mugs on coasters bearing the Archduke's famous handlebar mustache image. I heard my dad's cheer—to your health—*Na Zdravi*.

Tomáš and his nephews Martin and Ondřej Matějka provided English translation as needed, but mostly tender smiles and affectionate hugs bridged any gap there was in understanding. Pavel brought extensive family tree documents; Hanuš shared the Terezín Memorial Book, which detailed what was known at their print date of what happened to the multitude of people who were a part of the Terezín story. The book traced my grandparents to Lublin, Poland. As experts Peter Black and Robert Kuwalek had told me, they likely became part of a transport group with Bohemian Jews sent on to Sobibor. No official record exists to confirm precisely where, when, and how they perished.

Věra produced an abundance of old pictures and articles about her Benešov mayor grandfather. As I looked at one photo, a story came rushing back. Amazingly, I possessed a formal black top hat in my Orlando home, given to my dad by Uncle Jaroslav. It was worn by the Benešov mayor, František Marik (Jaroslav's father), when Otto Franz Joseph, the brother of Archduke František Ferdinand d'Este, made an appearance in Dad's hometown. Otto made an official visit to Benešov on behalf of the Austria-Hungarian Emperor after their fishponds' dikes failed and flooded the area, killing about fifty people. Věra gave me two gifts—a black-and-white drawing by a Terezín survivor that she knew and an etched metal plate tracing Benešov's skyline. Tomáš translated that this plate had earlier belonged to cousin Franta Ohrenstein, who, after the war, married Věra's older sister. I thought of how I came to know Franta through my dad's stories and how my father would have loved Věra's gesture of kindness.

Nephews Martin and Ondřej showed a picture of themselves as young boys holding a plastic model of an American Space Shuttle, given to them by my father on a long-ago trip to their home. For Dad's service as a physician to the Space Coast's early scientists, engineers, and astronauts, he'd been honored with a "Space Pioneer" certificate, which proudly propelled him to share his related experiences. Tomáš brought a picture of my father and himself smiling broadly at Orlando's Walt Disney World, wearing Mickey Mouse and Donald Duck hats. This trip to America just after the Iron Curtain crumbled, and he and his compatriots became free to travel the world in 1989. It was representative of several visits to America by Czech relatives in which my father joined them to show off his adopted country.

After almost three hours of shared stories about our intertwined lives, I led a toast—a heartfelt thank-you for a day that was more than I had dreamed. With my hand placed over my heart and Tomáš translating as I went along, I told them how I knew all our family members from the great beyond were cheering us on, no doubt also holding their aperitif glasses high.

With everyone as my guest choosing whatever they wanted from the menu, I smiled as I noticed familiar Czech favorites such as mushrooms stuffed with pork fillet medley, medallions of rabbit served with horseradish, cabbage, and boiled potatoes, and spicy pork goulash. Topping off the lunch was the surprise Tomáš and I had arranged. Delivered with great fanfare by the waiter arrived a fruit-enhanced birthday cake for Hanuš and Pavel. We sang "Happy Birthday" in Czech and English as we washed the cake down with Becherovka, a powerful Czech 'firewater' liquor that serves as a tonic in good and bad times.

Led by former tour guide Tomáš, the eighteen of us walked together on gray cobblestone streets to the nearby Benešov Jewish cemetery, passing by the thirteenth-century ruins of a monastery chapel destroyed by the Hussites. As I walked arm in arm with Věra, passing through a gate supported by a long stone wall, we arrived at a finely maintained red-brick Holocaust memorial museum at the cemetery. A sign in Hebrew commented on human fate in general: "From dust to dust." In the act of respect, before we entered the museum, Hanuš donned his yarmulke.

My father's name and his childhood friend Dr. Ella Baumgartner Traub—both financial contributors to the museum's restoration-were displayed on a plaque. A museum caretaker said my dad had paid for the cemetery's upkeep for many years. Inside were two rooms that explored the history of prominent Benešov citizens and gave information about the Benešov-Neveklov region, which endured universal evacuation of all villages from the Nazi change-over to SS Drill Training Grounds from 1942-45. Forced by the Nazis from their homestead, the Mařík family learned after the war; the German Army used their home and sawmill as a garrison hospital and practice yard.

The exhibition was devoted to the leading local Jewish citizens. Great-grandfather Alois Holzer's nineteenth-century role as a prominent businessperson was displayed on the wall via a fine sketch drawing of the Holzer home and store on the square. There, my father was born. Several other featured houses with the family name honoring their generation were familiar. Lists of Benešov citizens tortured and executed in concentration camps filled the museum walls. For a long time in front of Marie, Olga, and Arnošt Holzer's names, I was thinking of my father and what his fate might have been. Of the approximately five hundred Jews still living in Benešov when World War II broke out, only five survived the Nazis. One was Franta Ohrenstein, who married Věra's sister Otla.

Joanie looking at family names in Benešov Jewish Cemetery memorial, 2009

As we walked outside to the 1883 cemetery, rain began to drizzle, complementing our somber mood. Tomáš opened his bright blue umbrella. We passed the mass grave where thirteen French Jewish citizens, not from Benešov, were buried—machine-gunned to death by Nazis as the people sought water when their train transport stopped in early 1945 at the Benešov station. The Nazis were annoyed with the amount of time they took water at the fountain.

In the children's section, I looked for the graves of Arnošt's sisters, Elsa and Camilla, who died in 1892 at three and six years old from scarlet fever and diphtheria, two diseases that today no longer haunt the Czech lands. I could not find their names among the weathered stones, as I created in my mind a seven-year-old Arnošt standing alongside his grief-stricken parents, Alois and Marie, as the caretaker buried his sisters.

Inscriptions on tombstones were in Hebrew, German, and Czech. Among the gravestones, I recognized the names Schoenbaum, Ohrenstein, Fischer, Furth, and Orlík. All mentioned in letters or interviews. At last, I stood at the foot of my great-grandfather's massive black marble headstone, Alois Holzer—the namesake for my father's middle name. The gravestone served as a memorial also to his wife, Marie, and children who lost their lives in the Holocaust. A decade earlier, this place of honor was where my cousin Tomáš placed some of my father's ashes. In 2000, Tomáš and wife Lida attended my parents' memorial service in Melbourne. He transported some ashes from Florida in an old film canister that had belonged to my dad during his years in China. A fitting vessel to take a piece of him home to Bohemia.

Holzer Family Headstone, Joanie with Kelly and Derick, Benešov, 2018

From the cemetery, Tomáš drove us by Konopiště castle, now a major tourist attraction. Next, we traveled the lush rolling countryside to Neveklov, where the longtime homestead of the Mařík family awaited us. Perfectly preserved from the 1940s art deco period, it now serves as a weekend getaway for Jaroslav and Valda's descendants. As we gathered around a vintage kitchen table, drinking the famous herbal liqueur Becherovka and eating mouthwatering Kolache pastry, we told stories with Tomáš as a translator. Nearby were eight cactus plants in the kitchen window, two of which Tomáš pointed out as original plants belonging to Aunt Valda. Had Olga shared my father's cacti gift with her sister-in-law? Or perhaps when Arnošt left the last letter with his sister, he gave her the cacti for safekeeping.

Pavel asked Tomas to translate a funny story from his parents about my father after graduating from Medical School. Dad had gone with a group of friends to a Prague Cinema, Lucerna. Just as the movie got underway in the darkened theater, the lights came back on, and a voice rang out:

"Dr. Valdik Holzer. Dr. Valdik Holzer. Please report to the front desk. We need your assistance."

Realizing he had a unique, dramatic opportunity to let everyone in the theater know he was now a doctor, my father had paid a theater employee to page him. Pavel said it was the finest example of self-promotion he ever heard. Hearty laughter overtook the room.

Věra answered the question as to why Arnošt and Olga got married at Hotel Bristol in Prague, something I guessed about after studying their wedding certificate. She remembered the hotel had a reliable connection somehow to Benešovians within the Žižkov district. Whenever Věra and her relatives traveled to Prague, Hotel Bristol was their small yet elegant gathering place. She described how my father and Franta Ohrenstein were Red Seven members, an artistic club where each nurtured their creative spirit. Of my Dad, she remembered his caricatures of Charles University professors and friends.

Libor, son of Pavel, brought a "perfect soldier" helmet to the kitchen table. Tomáš translated the accompanying story detailing the hardship young Pavel endured after the Communists took over. Upset over their family's capitalist-leaning history from previously operating their sawmill, the Communists sent teenager Pavel to hard labor in a mine. He performed admirably and was awarded this helmet with a "perfect soldier" emblem.

Libor, now a tunnel engineer as well, encouraged his father to put the helmet on. Sure enough, grinning from ear to ear, Pavel obliged. We all laughed until our sides ached; the rhythm of life continued. It was heartwarming yet stunning to think about all this family had endured, yet they still laughed. Then I remembered—they were Czech. *And so was I.*

Before everyone left Neveklov that day, I wandered around the garden beside the house, imagining what it was like when my father visited in the good days before the Nazis arrived in March 1939. As Tomáš held his umbrella to shield my bright red dress from raindrops, the history of my father awakened in me. I began to imagine events and experience sensations at stops along my writing journey. At the Holzer house on the small Benešov square where Dad entered the world, I could feel Olga's excruciating labor pains on the hot summer day in 1911. I embodied Dad's joy in 1937 as he stood at the graduation podium accepting his Charles University diploma, becoming a physician in the presence of family and friends who cheered for his dream come true. In his gray army riding breeches in late March 1939, I observed Dad write fake orders in scribbled Czech to leave his Nazi-held Czechoslovak army unit, adding bureaucratic stamps to trick the Nazi guard who let him pass through the gate on his way to freedom.

Next, a train conductor walked by me as he whispered to Dad, "I'll open the train car's door early to allow you to evade the Gestapo and slip back to your parents' Prague apartment." Two months later, in late May 1939, I watched Dad at the central train station in Prague, filled with uncertainty, as he boarded the car on his way to China via Paris and Marseille, France, and thousands of nautical miles. As if I was standing by his trembling self, I watched the train's steam encircle Arnošt as Olga's fresh tears hit the moist ground as they bid painful farewells. Goodbyes in the air, as neither side knew it was their last. He and I were not prepared to deal with the separation.

Moving along, Dad's smiling face greeted me from the Chenonceaux ship captain's steering wheel somewhere in the Indian Ocean on his way to safe harbor in Shanghai. I was reminding myself of some positive aspects of the separation as we were about to see the world when suddenly, a Japanese colonel holding a rifle was illuminated beside us in a filthy train car in the vast interior of China. Puzzled by the "water" drops falling on his head from a basket above, the soldier was unaware they were urine from dad's hidden puppies. As months passed in a second, I sat beside Dad on the fateful train ride to Peking in August 1940, just days before my missionary mom arrived back in her homeland.

In Peking of old, Beijing of new, I heard Dad's first carefree laugh in years as his first chance meeting cemented my mom's immediate and everlasting affection for him. I witnessed the magic just eight days later, on September 20, 1940, when he lightly nudged a beggar to the side so he could finish his marriage proposal on a dusty Peking street. Mom's heartfelt acceptance, "Yes, I would like to be married to you," echoed in the wind of the Neveklov garden as if it had carried her life-changing words across the world, true music for my ears.

But the landmarks on my journey were not entirely over. After a vision of crossing the Pacific and time spent in California, I saw red, white, and blue flags waved before my eyes as my father and mother danced with excitement. In Lafayette, Indiana, he just received notice of American citizenship on April 27, 1944, and subsequent orders by the American military assignment of doctors to work on South America's oilfields U.S. war effort. Soon sunshine peeked through the clouds as he was awarded the chance to help defeat the villainous enemy that had consumed his world, serving as a doctor in oil fields where all the oil was going to the war effort. When the time capsule suddenly pitched, I realized where I was, as a light seemed to stream through the cloud above to the patch of earth where I stood. I heard my father reading Arnošt's last letter on the Ecuadoran porch overlooking the Pacific, the sea of peace. Lastly, as my dad's image drifted away, I saw myself sitting on the floor in 2008 beside the wooden desk he'd made the year I was born in Chattahoochee, Florida. My hands held the precious letter that Dad received that day in Ecuador and later hid it away in the desk. The message shared in that letter had been waiting to meet the world.

After my journey through time, I took the opportunity to kneel on my paternal ancestral ground and touch the moist earth that held my father's spirit along with the extended Czech family he adored. At long last, I was ready to fulfill his dream of writing his story.

Now, as more than a decade of research and discovery has passed by, my first two books, *Adventurers Against Their Will* and *My Dear Boy*, as well as *Steadfast Ink*, have allowed me to share many stories and truths Dad bestowed upon me through what he left behind. My father didn't watch from the shadows. He did as his father asked, going beyond the self, finding ways to look after one another, as if we are: one humanity.

Dad's experiences serve as a *useable history* for both of us—a term historians employ when the past provides a meaningful lesson for the greater good.

Czech Family Reunion, Benešov 2018

Epilogue: To Know the Place

"*I sat upon a promontory*
High above the sea.
And out upon the distant stage
The showers danced for me.

They spread a rainbow carpet,
To join the sea and sky
And, from my private rock seat,
I watched the Heavens cry."

RUTH ALICE HOLZER,
Antigua Island, 1975

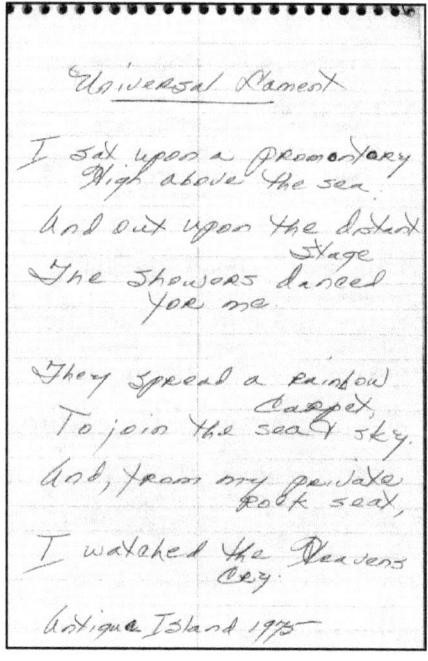

"Universal Lament"

My grandparents Arnošt and Olga mentioned 'Providence' several times in letters to their son, and it has played a repeated role in my experience. Springing from Latin roots, Providence is defined in the Merriam-Webster Online Dictionary as: *Divine guidance and care; God conceived as the power sustaining and guiding human destiny.*

I remain at a loss as to why the "guided human destiny" for my grandparents and so many others—around six million Jews and five million non-Jews—led to such an unimaginable result. But I have come to believe that Providence led me to tell their story, which allowed them to come alive again for remembrance and universal learning.

Because my parents departed this earth without a word about what lay hidden in those lacquer boxes and that Florida-pine desk, I will never be sure why my father kept secret his collection of letters, photographs, and personal mementos. I can only speculate that if Dad brought them out to discuss, he would have felt pressured to answer questions he never wanted to face with his adult children. My mother protected my father just as his parents had protected him so long ago. The Holocaust was the most formative event of his life. Because these items were the only tangible representation of loved ones left behind and most lost forever, it was beyond consideration that my father would have thrown them away.

My dad knew the letters would offer closure to a story he could never bring himself to tell. The collection is the greatest offering he could have given me beyond his spoken words. My journey set in motion by the letters, just like my father's from the familiar to the unknown, is unlike anything else I've ever experienced. Along the way, I found answers to questions I never knew existed until I read the letters.

T. S. Elliot wrote of this phenomenon beautifully:

With the drawing of this Love and the Voice of this Calling

We shall not cease from exploration
And the end of all our exploring
Will be to arrive where we started
And know the place for the first time . . . [9]

I now know the place of my life. Words cannot protect us from harsh realities—lives shattered, or worse, by atrocities and war—but when I read the letters in the treasure trove, I am with my father and mother then and now. From lives filled with sorrow and joy, they consciously decided to live with light, not darkness. The most exemplary legacy they left their children was the lens through which they looked at the world, one filled with a vision of faith that illuminates the human family's oneness. My grandfather Arnošt left us the legacy of living within that family, each doing our best to help humanity.

In the fall of 2011, Roger and I returned to Prague in conjunction with an American Friends of the Czech Republic (AFoCR) event. We saw history come full circle with the dedication of a newly reproduced U.S. President Woodrow Wilson statue outside the city's Main Railway Station. It was within steps of where my father said his last goodbye to his parents in 1939. The original monument by sculptor Albín Polášek was erected on July 4, 1928. It was torn down on the orders of Reinhard Heydrich in 1941 after the United States entered World War II. Americans of Czech and Slovak descent

---

[9] Eliot, Thomas Stearns. *Four Quartets*. United Kingdom: Harcourt Brace Jovanovich, 1988. Page 59.

American Friends of the Czech Republic (AFoCR), Walk to Freedom

funded the new statute. My brother and I joined their ranks as financial supporters with a marble plaque honoring my father's name on the accompanying Walk to Freedom.

Subsequent trips to my father's homeland in 2014 and 2018 reinforced what I already knew. The blood that runs through my veins and my descendants will always connect us to our Czech Bohemian roots. The people, places, and culture of our past profoundly influence our perspectives, even though we may not be aware of the impact.

In 2018, for the 100th-anniversary celebration of the formation of Czechoslovakia, Roger and I were accompanied to Prague by my daughter Kelly, her husband Andy, and my son Derick. My father's story was selected as one of eighteen people featured in a Czech

National Trust exhibit, *Ticket to the New World*. Scattered throughout the city, each venue showcased extraordinary life stories of internationally renowned and not-so-famous Czechoslovaks forced to leave their home country at the beginning of the Second World War.

With photos and other documents from that period, Dad's exhibit in the Werich Villa on Kampa Island in the heart of historic Prague featured letters sent from several continents by the Jewish exiles who corresponded with my father. An *Adventurers Against Their Will* presentation by his proud daughter—me—with an audience that included relatives of some of Dad's letter writers ensured a magical experience. In a later event summary, I realized how Dad's story resonates: "*Joanie Schirm, an American writer and the daughter of Oswald Holzer, who traveled all the way from the United States to share her memories of her father, was a very emotional experience for everyone who attended.*"

Joanie, Derick, and Kelly in Prague, 2018

The trip offered a chance to show my adult children around Prague, visiting many of their grandfather's favorite haunts accompanied by endless recitations of stories he'd told me. Among my favorite locales was a sunset dinner and beers (*tekutý chleb*, meaning liquid bread) shared at Café Manes, nestled beside the swan-laden Vltava River overlooking the stone Gothic Charles Bridge. As I repeated Dad's tales, vivid images popped into my head of him and his college-aged friends' enjoyable times debating the day's issues, playing cards, and, with enthusiasm, drinking pivo before the Nazis turned everything to darkness.

Spirits lifted as we enjoyed a family reunion in Benešov and Prague's unique joy at the world-famous Astronomical Clock at the Old Town Square. As musicians, puppeteers, and fire-eating jugglers circled around us, on the hour, a skeleton named Death rang the bell. Immediately, all the other clock figures shook their heads side to side, signifying their unreadiness "to go," exemplifying my feelings exactly whenever I had to say goodbye to Prague. But after this trip, with my children fully connected as I was to this marvelous ancestral land, I was ready.

At last, I could tell my father what I wasn't prepared to say to him before:

> I am so proud of you for how you lived out your father's wish.
> Your burden is buried.
> May you rest in deserving peace, my dear dad.
> Amen.

Dr. O. A. Holzer, 1967

APPENDIX

Synchronicities From My Writing Journey

The Merriam-Webster dictionary defines synchronicity as "the coincidental occurrence of events... that seem related but are not explained by conventional mechanisms of causality." During research toward the publication of *Adventurers Against Their Will* and *My Dear Boy*, I've recorded numerous intertwined events that, by this definition, involve a cosmic wink that I can't explain. Whether it's luck, karma, Divine timing, or a miracle, the Universe has repeatedly handed me the goods. There is no other way to explain it.

For over a decade, I've been immersed in a labor of love writing about my father's adventurous life before, during, and after World War II. I've employed every modern research tool I could find to uncover intimate and previously unknown details. From which the stories are sourced, the Holzer collection was described by the United States Holocaust Memorial Museum's former Chief Archivist Henry Mayer as one of "the largest and most comprehensive personal collections I've seen for some time." The National World War II Museum, along with Holocaust Education Centers and other educators worldwide, feature *Adventurers Against Their Will* and *My Dear Boy* on recommended reading lists. The lesson plans, prepared by Echoes & Reflections and USHMM Fellow teachers, are available free to teachers on my website: www.joanieschirm.com.

At the heart of the Holzer Collection, four hundred multi-paged letters, written between 1939 and 1946 by seventy-eight writers (primarily Czech), are postmarked from four continents. The letters personalize history in a way that's hard to do through documents where the emotions are scrubbed away like birth, marriage, military, and death certificates—all items I've gathered in my quest to understand and confirm facts.

As translated letters arrived, I worked night and day to solve who these letter writers were and their relationships to my dad. Using online search engines, telephone, personal interviews, and searching through Czech, American, German, Israeli, Chinese, and British archives, I identified 300 names mentioned in the messages.

As their voices grew distinct, they recounted an on-the-ground poignant and often disturbing view of the tumultuous world unfolding around them in what we would later call "Shoah" or "Holocaust." Seventy years later, my job turned to locate the letter's authors or their surviving descendants. As the puzzle pieces fit together, I learned over and over that if I remained open to the unexpected, synchronicities would emerge.

The Door Knocker

The end of 2007 was a reflective time for me. I was in the process of selling my stake in the Orlando engineering company I founded seventeen years earlier, and at long last, I would transition to a writer's life. The anticipation was high. So was my anxiety level about this significant life change. To reduce my stress, I tried to concentrate on a string of daily activities. I spent the entire 2008 New Year's Eve morning dismantling holiday decorations for their annual storage in a small, already crowded closet under a staircase.

My husband, Roger's job, was to pack the decorations in the closet among other household goods as best he could. As he arranged one box upon another in the crowded space, he observed, "You know you really need to store your mother and grandmother's antique silver pieces in a better way. Two sharp prongs from the old serving fork are sticking out of the side of the bag. Be careful."

It was apparent when I put the silver away after a recent family dinner I'd jammed too many pieces into one of my mom's old brown felt bags. Now the fork revealed my haste. I felt a twinge of guilt, but more important, Florida outdoors was calling me. I needed to go for my daily walk.

As I'd done each morning for the preceding year in preparation for writing my dad's story, I grabbed one of his interviews recorded in 1989 and listened as I strolled. The recordings were my attempt to capture tales he'd told endlessly during my youth. As a decade had passed, I'd forgotten a lot and was refreshing my memory to see what I might incorporate into my books.

My neighborhood hikes over old brick streets provided

opportunities to experience a kind of time-travel back to the mystical places my father discussed. As his voice transported me, I disappeared into another era and met relatives whose DNA created my features and whose blood ran through my veins. Dad's words let me live through his 1930s and 1940s wartime escapades plus accounts from his 1950 and 1960s medical practice in Melbourne, Florida, where I grew up.

Depending on the cassette, I might find myself on a steam-puffing train with armed Japanese soldiers occupying China in 1940 or, the next moment, with a rocket scientist my father knew and treated as a patient in the 1960s, shaping the nation's emerging space program in Central Florida. As the pain of the Holocaust kept my dad from telling me much about his parents, stories from his happy childhood provided me with a welcome, magical glimpse of what my grandparents Arnošt and Olga were like. I never tired of hearing my father's lingering Czech-accented voice as my feet trod in Orlando, but my heart traveled all over the world encountering adventure.

During the previous months of periodic listening, I had tended to dwell on the history of my father's early years in Bohemia or China. However, on December 31st, I felt like something different, so I chose a more contemporary, upbeat period from my old hometown. Based on the title my dad wrote on the tape, "Melbourne," I thought it would contain interesting cases from his medical practice.

As I walked the first two blocks, I listened to unusual descriptions of unusual patients. I met the famous architect Henry Hornbostel, who designed several iconic New York City bridges and the Carnegie Mellon University campus. Due to some prior military service, my dad called Henry "Major" Hornbostel. He wintered in Melbourne Beach, where he had chosen my father as his doctor. Like with so many other patients, they developed a friendship. Next, on the recording, my dad switched briefly to recounting the Space Age that dawned near our home and his role as physician to Werner von Braun, among other German scientists facilitating the development of Cape Kennedy (later Kennedy Space Center). Dad had volunteered as he spoke German and was already doing employment physicals for many of the space program's companies. (Von Braun was known to have been a Nazi, but Dad never mentioned that sordid fact.)

Abruptly on the recording, my father changed subjects. Shifting to a somber tone, I heard him say: *"In 1963, we went back to Czechoslovakia for the first time after the war. This was a trip of mixed emotions. My family in Czechoslovakia had vanished during the war. Only the Mařík's family survived . . ."*

From previous times I'd listened to his recordings, I'd gotten used to my father jumping around in time, unbound by chronological order. But on that morning promenade, I hadn't expected to stroll into this point in his life. When he had finally returned to his native land, it was controlled by the Communist Party from behind what was known as the "Iron Curtain." My mood sobered as my pace slowed upon the uneven bricks beneath my feet.

My dad's voice continued in a bittersweet tone as he conveyed information about the Mařík family before and after the Nazi occupation ended in 1945. After this long and involved story, my father described how he'd smuggled my grandmother's hidden silver out when he and my mom visited the Mařík's in 1963—some of the same silver pieces I'd just stored away. My dad followed with descriptions of the communist occupation and its impact on the Mařík family and others he knew.

As my feet continued to traverse streets lined with large shady oaks strewn with Spanish moss, I listened to fascinating tales from 1963 about my father's reunion with old friends and classmates from Charles University Medical School. Twenty-five years had elapsed since they'd last been together as young adults before the Nazis arrived.

One of these friends was his professor of chemistry, Dr. Jan Sula. After WWII, Dr. Sula married Helen Krulis-Randa, a debutante who attended their medical school dances. Before the war, Helen's noble old family had manor houses and castles in south-central Bohemia. Her grandfather was a member of one of the nineteenth-century governments of Emperor Franz Josef of the Austro-Hungarian Empire.

In each major province like Bohemia, a representative of the Emperor's government was known as a "Home Minister." Her father was one of these representatives and president of a stainless-steel cartel in Prague. When the Communists came to power after World War II, they picked him up and incarcerated him in Prague's jail. The poor man was a severe diabetic, and of course, the diet he received in prison was not precisely a diabetic diet. They refused to give him his insulin, and he died in the Communist jail. The Communists nationalized the estates and manor houses. In 1963 when my father and mother arrived, Helen's mom lived in a small, cold-water flat in the old part of Prague.

Since my dad had known her before the war, Helen wanted him and my mother to see her while they were in Prague, so they went for a visit one afternoon. It was a painful experience for my father. She was of the generation of his parents. Once again, he was reminded of all that was lost. This cultured older woman lived in a one-room apartment, a rather large room with a small kitchen and outside toilet, used by a half dozen people with similar flats on the floor.

Helen's mother had furnished her apartment with the most beautiful antiques from their old castles, somehow miraculously saved through the war. She used three large wardrobes to divide this room into a living room and bedroom. She still had a collection of beautiful antique porcelain and gorgeous Renaissance paintings hung on the dingy walls.

My parents told Mrs. Krulis-Randa, they were going to Vienna after visiting Prague. She asked my father whether he would deliver a letter to 'her friend' Duke Schwarzenberg. The Duke was still living in the Schwarzenberg Palace, which had opened in 1725. As it happened, one wing of this grand old palace was converted into a hotel, and my parents had serendipitously reserved a room for their upcoming stay in Vienna. They agreed to the mission of mercy. Before they left Prague, Helen Sula delivered her mother's letter for Duke Schwarzenberg to my parent's hotel.

After my father had described that he'd agreed to act as a courier, he went on to tell several other stories about their train trip from Prague to Vienna. I listened, anxious to know if the letter made it to the Duke. At last, he described their arrival in Vienna at the Schwarzenberg Palace.

I asked at the reception desk where I could see Duke Schwarzenberg. They looked at me kind of suspiciously. Finally, someone said, "Why do you want to see the Duke?" I stated that I had a letter to deliver to him. Arrangements were made for the following day to go to see the Duke. I was informed that I should wear a dark suit when I went to see the Duke. Ordinarily, I travel around Europe in flannel slacks and a sports jacket, but I always carry some better suits so we can go to the opera or something like that. I got all dressed up, shined my shoes, and went for the appointment.

At the palace entrance, I was met by a footman in the proper uniform. He led me upstairs to the second floor, where I was met by the Duke's secretary, a middle-aged gentleman in a dark cutaway suit. He instructed me how to behave on my entrance to the Duke's study. I was supposed to enter and walk to the desk where he was sitting. I should stand up behind the desk but not say anything until the Duke addressed me. I followed his instructions, but as soon as I entered the room, the Duke got up, walked toward me, and shook my hand. Then he took me to his desk and asked me to sit down.

I handed him the letter, which he immediately opened and started to read. He started making all kinds of comments in German. Then he turned to me and started talking in perfect Oxford English. He asked me how things were in Prague, whether I met his cousin. When I told him I got the letter through Mrs. Krulis-Randa, he said, "Well, how is the old girl?" After a short conversation, he said, "I detect some accent in your English. Do you speak German?" I said "yes," and from then on, we conversed in German. I stayed there for about ten minutes. Then we got up, and he walked with me to the door and shook hands again.

Recalling this exchange with great pleasure, my father closed with: "And so that is how I ended my audience with the Duke

Schwarzenberg."

As often happened when I listened to the recordings, I walked home feeling as if I'd had an excellent morning conversation with my dad. Although some of our time together had sad aspects, most of it made me joyful for what life entails—extraordinary and ordinary life events.

When I returned home, I decided to take some constructive action to store Mother's silver pieces more respectfully. I pulled the felt brown bags from the closet and placed them on the dining room table, carefully removing each piece. I enjoyed thinking about how some of these were my Grandmother Olga's secretly buried silver pieces. They'd been hidden in Uncle Jaroslav and Aunt Valda's orchard until after retrieval following the war. Somehow, they went undiscovered by the rotten Nazis as they carried out shooting practice standing atop them, a small piece of justice in a world mad with injustice.

In the 1950s, it was customary for my mom to wrap her silver pieces with white tissue paper carefully; she believed that the tissue would protect them from tarnishing. Upon my inheritance of this share of family heirlooms, I couldn't bring myself to dispose of the tissues, so the paper remained in place. Within the two felt bags were various items I'd never used—old silver cigarette lighters and small sugar plates. It had been a long time since I'd polished anything in the bags. I decided it was time to get to work.

As I organized them on our dining room table, I came across something I hadn't noticed before. In a thicker-then-usual piece of white paper was something brass, not silver. As I removed it, I held what appeared to be an old door knocker. On the front top half, carved in great detail, was a man riding a horse. The horse and his rider were perched atop an emblem of sorts with the number "8" engraved on it. Holding this object in my hands, rubbing its fine brass, I found myself smirking. Apparently, my father must have "lifted" this doorknocker at some time in his extensive world travels. It seemed uncharacteristic for him and was not my mother's style. Staring at the object for a long minute, I wondered how it made it into the silver collection.

And then, as it happened, I turned the doorknocker around to look at its back, and there, etched in the brass in black letters, was:

Hotel Palais
Schwarzenberg

I gasped; my body shook.

Sitting nearby, my husband asked what happened. I described the recording I'd just listened to while walking and what I now held in my trembling hands.

Roger grinned as he calmly replied, "That is clearly your father telling you that you need to get busy writing his stories." And thus, I began writing.

The Lost Brandy

Not exactly synchronicity, the following story provides a little background to the hidden silver. In early 1940, while occupying my father's homeland, the Nazis announced to Czech citizens that they were required to turn over precious valuables such as gold, platinum, and silver. Their treasures were to be sold at a discount to a particular company dealing in Jewish property that had been confiscated in various ways.

Wanting no part of that, my grandparents secretly gave their silver and jewelry to my grandfather's sister Vala (my dad called 'Aunt Valda') and brother-in-law Jaroslav to bury in a large orchard beside their Neveklov sawmill and homestead. Along with the valuables, Uncle Jaroslav included a rare bottle of brandy to be opened in celebration when the war ended. Uncle Jaroslav made a map based on the trees' locations to mark where everything was buried. Soon, the Nazi forces kicked out the residents of Neveklov and occupied the Jaroslav home, using it as a garrison hospital. Legend has it that the Nazis practiced there to get ready for their Belgium invasion because the rolling landscape was similar. The Nazis sent Uncle Jaroslav (who wasn't Jewish) and his oldest son Jiri (George) from Neveklov to two separate forced labor camps.

After six years of occupation, the war had finally ended by the summer of 1945, and the family of four returned Neveklov—their property was severely damaged, and the orchard burned down. With the trees gone, the map to the buried goods had been rendered useless. Over the years, family members dug here and there and finally recovered the silver collection. But, they never found the brandy.

As my father said later when telling the story, having lost his parents in the Holocaust and forty-two other relatives, the brandy was never meant to be found. With so many loved ones perished, there was no reason to celebrate.

Back to synchronicities . . .

World Pain

The experiences of discovery, receipt of the translation, and reading of Arnošt's final letter and altruistic wish that changed the course of my father's life also changed the course of mine. That moment when my son Derick and I read it is forever embossed on my memory. After getting almost no sleep the following Saturday night, I awoke with determination at 5:30 a.m. on Sunday to better organize the historical memorabilia in my writing room.

Before my work began, I dragged myself to my computer to check unopened emails I'd neglected for the past two days. The first message that popped up on the screen was the Visual Thesaurus Magazine 'Word of the Day.' With many other emails to read, I might not have bothered with this one had I not seen "*Weltschmerz*." Definition: "*Life got you down? If it comes from reflecting on the state of the world, at least you can give your ailment this name, a word on indefinite loan in English from German. Its components mean 'world pain,' and both have cognates in English: welt = world, schmerz = smart (the verb).*"

I sat up straight, frozen, as I stared at the screen. I reread the words: "world pain." It was precisely what I felt after reading Arnošt's letter!

I clicked on "weltschmerz" and was transported to the Visual Thesaurus website, which featured a diagram showing the definition of "world-weariness" and the description, "Sadness of thinking about the evils of the world." The sadness of thinking about the world's evils captured my moment and many to follow. The irony not lost on me that this German word precisely described my state of mind.

An Astrologer's Foresight

During the fall of 2012, when the publication of *Adventurers Against Their Will* was approaching, I visited an astrologer in hopes of learning what the future held for my debut book. Not knowing of my project, he told me April 3 would be a powerful date for me in 2013. "If you are going to launch something, that is the time." I found his use of the word *launch* quite intriguing and set April 3, 2013, as my book's release date.

That night, I woke up at 3 a.m. thinking about what he had said. That's when I remembered that April 3, 2008, was the date I received the translation of Arnošt's last letter to my dad.

Chance Encounter at American Center of US Embassy in Prague

In September 2014, in conjunction with the Czech language book launch of *Adventurers Against Their Will*, I was invited to speak at the American Center at the US Embassy in Prague. As I polished my PowerPoint presentation, rife with photographs and graphics of my book's star characters, I noticed a woman in her fifties or sixties wander into the room cradling some papers in her arms. I assumed she worked at the center. I'd been receiving technical assistance from an Embassy computer technician to prepare for my Power-Point on their screen. We'd paused briefly on a photograph of Frantisek "Franta" Schoenbaum/Šeba—the subject of Chapter 4 in my book. The woman stayed for a moment and then left. When the crowd later filled the room for my talk, I noticed this woman sitting in the front row.

Afterward, Eva Cieslarova (born Fridova)—introduced herself and told me her late father, Myrtil Frida (a film historian), was best friends with Franta Schoenbaum/Šeba. She said she'd been in the American Center for a meeting unrelated to my presentation when she spotted the photograph of Franta staring at her from the screen. That chance glance was why she'd stayed for my speech.

Eva told me that she rode on the back of Franta's motorcycle when she was probably sixteen years old. He was adventuresome and amusing with a dry sense of humor. When Franta died, she attended his memorial services and told me his ashes were spread on the Sázava River in

Central Bohemia, south of Prague. I promised to contact Franta's son, John, a seventy-plus-year-old professor living in New Zealand, as I was sure he would like to hear her memories. She gave me her email and promised to share Franta's later life stories. We had our photograph taken together—capturing one more synchronicity on the writing journey. Within the next few months, John and his son— Dayton, who had become interested in family history—shared stories and promised to meet Eva in person later in the Czech lands.

Benešovian, Linda Vlasak

In 2013, I was introduced by email to Linda Vlasak by a Czech researcher, Petr Šraier, involved in Geni.com's genealogical research site.

Linda is the Veselý family's granddaughter, neighbors across the small square in Benešov when my father and his Holzer family resided there before WWII. In her late 80s, when we met, Linda lived in Kansas with her daughter. Upon our introduction, I mailed her a copy of *Adventurers Against Their Will*. We soon struck up a long-distance friendship culminating in a 2015 meeting at the home she shares with her daughter Marion.

From the moment we connected, Linda offered her help via her keen knowledge of Benešov—both the place and people. At one juncture, I asked her to identify faces in a group photograph welcoming the first Czechoslovak President Tomas Masaryk to Benešov I'd received from my cousin Tomas Mařík. Linda had told me earlier her late grandfather was a close friend of Czecho-

 slovakia's first president. Linda took one look at the photo and immediately telephoned me to say she knew the woman at the group's center: it was her young mother. Standing in the mix was Uncle Jaroslav's father, the Mayor of Benešov, holding the black hat Jaroslav had given to my father that now sat in my writing room.

Over the years of my research and trips to Prague, the young man, Petr, who introduced me to Linda, became a great ally in the quest to learn about the Jews of Benesov. Due to Petr's efforts, three brass cobblestones, known as Stopersteine, literally "stumbling stones," were installed in front of the Holzer house and store in Benesov.

The Stolpersteine project started in 1993 when German artist Gunter Demnig placed the first 'stones' in Cologne in 1994. When in 1998 the project began in the Czech Republic, Petr helped spread the word, sharing the news with me in America. Petr made it possible for the Holzer memories to live where they spent their lives with stones placed where my father walked for the first almost three decades of his life.

In 2018, my beloved children, Kelly and Derick, and my husband Roger were able together to see the memories placed where my father called home. The small brass plaques bear the names of my great-grandmother and grandparents, the year of their birth, and the date of Nazi transport to their deaths. The 'stumbling stone' makes us pause and remind those that pass by, my relatives used to live there and, simply because they were Jewish, became victims of the Nazis.

The Peiping Chronicle—1946

In 2016, to understand the political situation surrounding my father's 1946-47 return trip to China more fully, I launched more research. I was primarily studying his employer's role, the United Nations Relief and Rehabilitation Administration (UNRRA), and their vast relief effort initiative in China just after WWII. When Dad arrived, the Chinese civil war between the Nationalist and Communist factions pulled the United States in different directions through raging disagreement in the US government and political circles. All sides were attempting to determine what America's role should be and which army they should support. The crippling effects of eight years of war, including devastation from Japanese warfare, had left China in chaos. My father had signed on for the world's first operational international relief organization carried out simultaneously across Europe and China. Dad set out to offer meaningful involvement and to share what medical services he could offer.

Because of Dad's experience six years earlier as a refugee physician in China and his ability to speak the language, he was sent as a General Surgeon to help rehabilitate war-torn hospitals. From a 1989 interview, I knew he'd been assigned to General George Marshall's Cease-Fire 12 team for some time, housed at their headquarters in Shanghai. Most stories he told me were light-hearted adventure tales. A few showed the danger of the escalating war, like when he traveled with a jeep brigade of Marines from Peking (Beijing) to Tientsin. A deadly shoot-out occurred between the Marines and Communist soldiers, but Dad, as always, managed to escape.

One day, I started wondering who was serving as the US Ambassador to China during that time and what their philosophy was. I found a Wikipedia summary about John Leighton Stuart, appointed to the position on July 4, 1946, one month after my father returned to China. Wikipedia revealed an interesting fact that Ambassador Stuart "was the last person to hold that position before the resumption of diplomatic relations between the two countries three decades later." The detail reminded me of the long schism between our nations. It also served as a reminder of my dad's deteriorating political situation before the Nationalist government fled Nanjing and the Communities forces took the capital city in April 1949. Stuart had maintained the US Embassy in Nanjing.

Ambassador Stuart worked in concert with the famous General George Marshall. My father had met the General in 1941 in Washington, DC, when he attempted to join the US Army while still technically an officer in the Czechoslovak Army, then in exile in England. Gen. Marshall had told Dad he needed to resign that (defunct) army, and "it would help if you would become a naturalized U.S. citizen."

In China, Ambassador Stuart and General Marshall were attempting to mediate between Nationalists and Communities. It was a challenging period in Chinese history. Both men were trying not to escalate America's involvement in their civil war. I found

Leighton-Stuart's background fascinating because he was born in China to American Christian missionaries like my mother.

The write-up intrigued me but failed to explain the philosophy and policies that Ambassador Stuart was taking forward. I began to wonder what my father might have known, and that spurred me to remember a file that my dad saved which included his UNRRA service papers. I retrieved it from my messy storage closet and leafed through the file. It was filled with old letters, formal UNRRA documents, and reports he'd issued to UNRRA superiors about his work at some hospitals. At the back of the file, I came across an old, yellowed newspaper—*The Peiping Chronicle* dated September 1, 1946. Peiping, like Peking, is an old Wade-Giles Romanization of the Mandarin postal system name for today's ancient yet modern city of Beijing.

On the front page, I noticed a headline: "Leighton Stuart Speaks at American Association: Shanghai, August 31, 1946." One paragraph caught my eye with words that still echo America's omnipresent stated mission.

"Most of those, both American and Chinese, who have written or spoken to me about the present task, have commented chiefly on its

difficulties. I had no illusion about these before I accepted the Ambassadorship, and since then, they have seemed to become even more complicated. But in another sense, my function is an easy one. By this, I mean that the American government and the American people want for China precisely those things which practically all Chinese, who think at all about such matters, themselves desire. These are national freedom and independence, internal unity and peace, economic progress and constructive development, and the establishment of a strong and genuinely democratic government. This is, to me, an extremely cheering consideration. It seems to be a superb instance of what Woodrow Wilson once described as 'friendly helpfulness to another nation.' The only problem—I am in no sense minimizing its perplexities- is how to achieve this clearly defined objective."

Synchronistic help had arrived once again from the universe. The old newspaper provided the answer I sought about what the ambassador saw as his mission: *peacemaker*. It is an essential element of our 'helpfulness' through the State Department on behalf of the American people and the value of freedom we hold dear.

Believe It or Not

One of the featured letter writers in *Adventurers Against Their Will* and *My Dear Boy* is Hana Winternitz Bell. My father's first cousin, Hana, fled to Great Britain in 1940. She survived the Holocaust although her Jewish parents Rudolf and Olga did not, both perishing at Auschwitz-Birkenau. After reading Hana's letters and her short memoir, I wondered what happened to the best friend she frequently mentioned: Eva.

Through a chance conversation with a Czech cousin, I discovered that Hana had a living nephew-through-marriage, Owain Bell, who resided in Great Britain. Canon Owain Bell (now retired) was ordained in 1972 as an Anglican priest. Since 1997, Owain had been the Vicar of St. Mary's, Kidderminster, where Richard Baxter, the famous seventeenth-century theologian, preached. Owain was a wealth of information about Hana. Before finding Owain, I had already located Hana's wedding certificate through a British marriage record database. But through live human contact—my favorite part of family history research—Owain brought the sterile wedding certificate information to life when he described her 1945 marriage to his uncle, Christopher Idris Bell.

"Idris was the first son of Sir Idris (Harold Idris in England) and Lady Winifred Bell," Owain wrote via email. "Sir Idris was a very distinguished scholar, Keeper of the Manuscripts at the British Museum and President of the British Academy . . . he was knighted in 1946."

Owain sent me a second short memoir which yielded many other jewels about Hana's life. Between her newsy letters and journal, I felt like she was right out of a tale by 19th Century British novelist Charlotte Bronte: *An earnest young woman toils through a series of jobs working as a humble domestic in the English countryside while dreaming of a better life.*

Raised in a wealthy Prague household, Hana is an excellent example of what many young European Jew's lives were like after receiving permission from the British government to work under a "domestic" permit. Upon her arrival, Hana served as a nanny and house cleaner. The positions saved her life, and she was forever indebted to the British. She died of natural causes in 2004 at the age of 83.

Owain also led me to Hana's daughter, Stephanie Bell. During a 2009 email exchange, Stephanie sent me a San Marino address for Hana's best friend, Eva Pacovska Gould. When she mailed it, Stephanie wasn't sure where San Marino was located in the United States, and I was too busy writing my books to research it. It would be two years before I decided to take a look online to see if I could locate Hana's friend. To my amazement, a notice yielded another address with her name that led me to believe there was a chance that Eva was still alive in San Marino, California. A house was for sale for $7 million, and the realtor's website allowed me to view the home virtually but did not provide any direct link to Eva.

Without an email address, I took a chance and wrote a letter to her on June 29, 2011, introducing myself and why I was writing. I asked if she was the same Eva I was searching for; if she was, would she be so kind as to share Hana memories and others from her Prague youth? Perhaps she'd even known my father? I included my email address and sent it off.

Six days later, I received this startling email response.

> *Dear Joanie,*
>
> *This past Saturday, I received your letter addressed to my mother at the San Marino, California address. My mother did indeed go by Pacovska and grew up in Prague, leaving for America in 1939.*
>
> *It is a most remarkable thing that your letter reached me. My mother, Eva, passed away two years ago last month, but she and my father had moved from the San Marino address in 2003. I had become friends with the current residents of our former family home in San Marino. They are*

moving to Oregon next month, so I stopped by to say goodbye, and, believe it or not, the postman delivered your letter while I was there.

I am copying my sister (also affectionately known as Joanie) on this letter with your letter attached. She is much more diligent than I in attending to family matters like these. She can tell you what information and photos we might have. Alas, my mother is not here to tell us what she may have remembered about Hana, but we may yet be able to piece some things together.

I look forward to learning more about your family. It was very exciting to receive your letter.

Best regards, Don (Donald P. Gould)

I can only assume a higher being made sure the letter was delivered by the US Mail on the day that Don happened to stop by. How else can one explain it? Soon Joan (Gould) Freed and I were sharing information, including a 1939 photograph of Eva and her parents, Bohumil Pocovsky and Helena Winter Pacovská, reminiscent of Hana's portrait with her parents taken the year before. Joan and I continued our correspondence. She and her family visited the Czech lands, and she sent me pictures from their trip.

My advice to genealogical investigators is that you approach your research in an open and receptive manner. Whenever possible, tie your effort to a dogged determination to find the story behind the documentation. There's deep satisfaction in realizing something extraordinary about the past sparked merely through a piece of paper. And don't be closed off to synchronicity!

Eva Pacovska (later Gould), 1939, with father Bohumil and mother Helena

Don Gould, sister Joan Gould Freed, on a family trip to Czech lands, 2019

More Than a Number – Holocaust in Bohemia and Moravia[10]

1 of 26,000

Oswald "Valdik" Holzer—one of 26,000 people who legally emigrated from Nazi-occupied Bohemia and Moravia 1939-41

44 of 118,310

Valdik Holzer's forty-four relatives—self-defined Jews living in the Protectorate of Bohemia and Moravia after the breakup of Czechoslovakia in 1939

44 of 73,603

Valdik Holzer's forty-four relatives along with Jews of Prague, Brno, Ostrava, Olomouc, and other towns of the Protectorate of Bohemia and Moravia deported to Terezín (Theresienstadt) 1941–44

---

[10] Accessed Source July 2021: United States Holocaust Memorial Museum. "Holocaust Encyclopedia: The Holocaust in Bohemia and Moravia." https://encyclopedia.ushmm.org/content/en/article/the-holocaust-in-bohemia-and-moravia

44 of 82,309 and 71,000

Valdik Holzer's forty-four relatives—of 82,309 Jews deported from the Protectorate of Bohemia and Moravia by Nazis; the Germans and their collaborators killed approximately 71,000. Valdik's parents, Arnošt and Olga Holzer, likely perished at Sobibor death camp in Poland.

14,000 of 118,310

By 1945, Protectorate Jews alive in the Protectorate

Biographies – Select Letter Writers and Family Members

Holzer, Oswald "Valdik" (1911-2000). Author's father. Correspondent and an adventurer against his will who preserved the hundreds of letters that form the basis for **Steadfast Ink** and companion volumes, **Adventurers Against Their Will** and **My Dear Boy**. Studied medicine at Charles University in Prague. Was serving as a doctor in the Czechoslovak Army when Germany invaded the Czech Lands in 1939. Escaped to China, where he married **Ruth Alice Lequear**. The couple moved to the United States in 1941. Settled in Florida in 1948, where he served as a Melbourne, FL family physician while living in a nearby beach town, Indialantic-by-the-Sea. Three children: Tom, Pat, and Joanie.

Holzer, Ruth Alice (nee Lequear) (1916-2000). Author's mother. Born in Yochow City, Hunan Province, China, the oldest child of American missionaries, Ruth Alice married "Valdik" in Peking (Beijing) in 1940. She died sixty years later, two days before Valdik died at the turn of the twenty-first century. She was a teacher, faith leader, and Elder at the Eastminster Presbyterian Church and Woman of the Year recognized for her leadership as children's choir director and Sunday school teacher. She was known for her community volunteerism in many aspects of her giving life. Three children: Tom, Pat, and Joanie.

Ballenberger, Karel "Bála" (1908-1996). One of the Mánes Café circle of Valdik's friends in Prague. A politically active lawyer, he encouraged Valdik to contribute anti-Hitler cartoons to the left-leaning Social Democratic Party's newspaper. Evacuated from Prague to London with help from the party as the German Army approached in 1939. Wife Milena (née Langer) stayed behind with their two children; all three later died in the Holocaust. Changed family surname to Bala. Injured in World War II in France. Remarried to Vera Judith "Mima" Lowenbach; raised two children, the late Ann Matyas and Nicholas, in Canada. Son Hugh Thompson by Joan Thompson lives in Great Britain.

Fischer, Rudolf "Rudla" (1901-1972). Valdik's first cousin. Successful banker. Fled from Prague to Italy, then to France, along with wife Erna (née Frenkel) and son Tom. Left family to serve with Czechoslovak Army in Exile in Britain. Remained there for the rest of his life. Erna divorced him, arranged passage to the United States, and remarried. Beginning in 2008, Rudla's son, Joanie's second cousin Tom (Fischer) Weiss, became her obsessive ally in the hobby of digging deep into family history.

Holzer, Arnošt (1885-1942) **and Olga (née Orlík) Holzer** (1888-1942). Valdik's parents. Both were born in the Czech Land of Bohemia in the Austro-Hungarian Empire. They were representative of the region's historically assimilated Jewish population. Lived in Benešov; relocated to Prague to be with Valdik when he enrolled at Charles University—transported by Nazis from Prague to Terezín on April 24, 1942. Killed by Nazis in late May 1942, likely at Sobibor death camp in eastern Poland. Never were able to meet Valdik's wife Ruth Alice or his grandchildren Tom, Pat, and Joanie.

Holzer, Marie (née Porges) (1862-1942). Valdik's grandmother. Born in Austro-Hungarian Empire. Transported by Nazis to Terezín on September 4, 1942. Died of pneumonia in Terezín on December 26, 1942. Her ashes were thrown by the Nazis, along with the remains of thousands of others, in the nearby Ohře River in an attempt to hide the evidence of Nazi atrocities. She never was able to meet her great-grandchildren.

Holm, Patricia Orlik (née Holzer) (1945-). Valdik and Ruth Holzer's oldest daughter. Born in Ecuador, she lives in Florida. A former teacher, community activist, first woman president of Taxpayer's Association of Indian River County, co-owner of Mid-Florida Ventures.

Holzer, Thomas Lequear (1944-). Valdik and Ruth Holzer's son. Born in Indiana, lives in California. Retired research geologist with the Earthquake Hazards Team of US Geological Survey in Menlo Park and former consulting associate professor at Stanford University; BSE in geological engineering from Princeton University in 1965, MS in hydrology in 1966 Ph.D. in geology in 1970 from Stanford University.

Kraus, Pavel "Paul" (1919-2014). One of Valdik's last friends to escape Prague; fled in April 1940, more than a year after the German occupation began. Sailed to Shanghai, China, and reconnected with Valdik, whom he was related by marriage (Rudi Winternitz was an uncle to both)—assisted in China by Leo Lilling. Resettled in America in 1941 and joined the US Army as a Ritchie Boy in the Military Intelligence Service, serving in Europe; helped liberate Dachau concentration camp and identify "the most dangerous man in Europe," Nazi Otto Skorzeny. Became an executive in the American distillery business along with older brother Frank Kraus. Interviewed in 2010 at age ninety-one by Joanie in Chicago for her book and *Adventurers Against Their Will*. Three children: Carole, Allen, and Ginny.

Lilling, Leo (1891-1978). Born in Vienna, Austria. Established Lilling & Company, successful import/export business in China, offices (and residences) in Hong Kong and Shanghai. Leo assisted Valdik immensely during his time in China. Rudi Winternitz's youngest brother married Leo's sister. Leo, his wife Melitta, and Melitta's brother Wilhelm Bless left Shanghai in 1952 and arrived in New York in 1956. Seeking further information.

Lilling, Melitta (née Bless) Leo married Austrian Melitta Bless in 1941. Losing all her possessions when the Nazis occupied Vienna,

Melitta migrated to Shanghai, where she learned to speak Czech, belonged to the Czechoslovak Circle, and swore loyalty to Czechoslovakia. Melitta (as Melitta Studio) hired Chinese women to stitch needlepoint canvases which she sent to Vienna to be made into evening purses—seeking further information.

Rebhun, Rudolf "Rudla" (1914-1988). Rudla's father was a friend of Arnošt Holzer in Prague when the German occupation began. In July 1939, he met Valdik in Shanghai. They became rowdy friends and later letter correspondents when Valdik moved to China's interior—immigrated to Australia in 1950—seeking further information.

Schirm, Joanie Holzer (1948-). Valdik and Ruth Holzer's youngest daughter. Born, raised, and living in Florida. Former Orlando business owner Geotechnical and Environmental Consultants, Inc.; chairperson of World Cup Orlando 1994; volunteer community activist including Leadership Cabinet for the Holocaust Museum for Hope & Humanity planned with creative partner USC Shoah Foundation for downtown Orlando; speaker, award-winning Author: *My Dear Boy: A World War Story of Escape, Exile, and Revelation*, and *Adventurers Against Their Will* and *Steadfast Ink*. Married to Roger Neiswender. Two children: Kelly Lafferman and Derick Schirm.

Schoenbaum (later Seba), Frantisek "Franta" (1910-2001). Valdik's childhood best friend and frequent correspondent whose letters showed consistent good humor, even in the darkest times.

Remained in occupied territory, shielded through the efforts of his non-Jewish wife Andula (née Nejedlá) until the final months of the war, when he was imprisoned at Terezín concentration camp. Andula arranged for their son Honza (John) to be hidden from the Nazis in the countryside. Second son Martin was born in 1945. All four survived the war, but the couple's marriage did not. Franta remained in Prague after their divorce. Andula moved to New Zealand with her sons and new husband. In 2018, Joanie and her husband, Roger, visited John in Wellington, New Zealand.

Schoenbaum, Karel (later Charles K. Sheldon) (1906-1958). Franta's older brother. He was working as a lawyer for the Škoda industrial complex when the Germans prepared to occupy. Escaped to London with wife Katka (née Graber). Earned a Ph.D. at Oxford University. Resettled in the United States in 1941 and changed the family name to Sheldon. Daughter Carol Sheldon Hylton, born in 1945, became a pivotal contact in attempts to trace the paths of the adventurers against their will.

Schoenbaum (later Sheldon) Pughe, Katherine "Katka" (née Graber). One of the two survivors interviewed for the companion book, *Adventurers Against Their Will*. Died on February 9, 2011, age ninety-three, with daughter Carol and grandson Kevin holding one of her hands. In 2009, Joanie interviewed Katka and remains friends with her daughter Carol.

Urbanek, Frantisek "Franta" (1894- ?). University of Prague financial accounting degree. Served in the Austro-Hungarian Army on the Russian front, 1914-18; POW; joined the independent Czechoslovak Legion as a lieutenant. Married twice; last in Charbin in 1922 to Vera Semjonovna Bastinskaja. Worked for the Commercial Head Office of Škoda Works in Prague; became director of branch offices in Vladivostok, Charbin, and Dairen (South Manchuria); in 1928, established an office in Peking and 1929 in Hong Kong, exporting to China sugar factories, power plants, etc. In 1934, managed commercial representations in Shanghai, Tientsin, Canton, and Hong Kong, including weapons made in Škoda Works in Plzeň (guns, tanks, ammunition, aircraft); exported light automatic weapons from Brno (Moravia) for the Army of China. In 1942, he left China for America, where he and Vera reunited with Valdik and Ruth Alice. Returned to Prague in 1946 and China (1946 and 1951-53); left in February 1948 for New York. Later lived in Santa Monica and Los Angeles. Seeking further information.

Wagner, Vladimír "Vláďa" (1911-2008). Valdik's close friend and fellow graduate of Charles University's medical school; later became a faculty member. Served as hematologist and pathologist for the state health department at several Prague hospitals during the war. An active participant of the Czech resistance during World War II, he was later jailed by the Communist regime. Years after the war, he told Valdik that medical personnel sabotaged blood administered to high-ranking Nazi official Reinhard Heydrich as he was recovering from an assassination attempt, leading to his death. Seeking more information.

Winternitz, Hana (1920-2004). Valdik's first cousin. Escaped alone to Holland, then to Great Britain in 1939. Worked as a domestic through much of the war before enrolling in business school on a scholarship. Married Christopher Idris Bell, a respected British family member who taught economic history at the University of Wales. Two daughters: Jennifer and Stephanie; Nephew Owain Bell. Owain and wife Kim have visited with Joanie and her husband, Roger, twice in America.

Holzer Family, 1955

Pat, Tom, Joanie, circa 1990s

As the late Secretary-General of the United Nations Dag Hammarskjöld's advice offers up in his book, *Markings*, we should always honor the present moment.

> *The present moment is significant, not as the bridge between past and future, but by reason of its contents, contents which fill our emptiness and become ours if we are capable of receiving them.*

As the third in my book series about my father's past, *Steadfast Ink* introduces the *present moment*. First referred by my beloved husband, Roger Neiswender, as "off the floor and out the door," *Steadfast Ink* preserves personal backstories that initially lived within draft manuscripts for *Adventurers Against Their Will* or *My Dear Boy-A World War II Story of Escape, Exile, and Revelation*. As those books grew to epic proportions, it was made clear by my editor Alice Peck that trimming needed to occur. Thus, clipped personal reflections fell by the wayside into a folder titled: *Backstories that reflect the present.*

After *My Dear Boy* met with success, Alice suggested a third volume that reaches back into the heart of my journey as I unraveled and fully understood what my complete mission needed to be as I shared this incredible tale with the world. The backstories became front stories, and *Steadfast Ink* joined the book series. Thank you, Roger and Alice.

For this book's acknowledgments, beyond this extraordinary, spiritual man of peace, the late Dag Hammarskjöld, I want to again thank my father for saving the Holzer Collection with its "*contents which fill our emptiness and become ours if we are capable of receiving them.*" My father, like my mother, always gave me unconditional love. They inspired everything I've done for leading a meaningful life. Because of their guidance, I became *capable of receiving* the lessons from our past.

Beyond Roger, my children, Kelly Lafferman and Derick Schirm, and brother Tom Holzer lead my list of loved ones that for over twelve years have repeatedly, to different degrees of prodding, suggested: "just get the job done." They, and my grandchildren Ty and Ava, understand our ancestors' messages and how important education is in changing our world. Thank you for your caring nature, patience, and encouragement.

To all who read my books and contemplate their meaning as we live in the present, thank you for your commitment to building a better world.

Peace.

About the Author

Joanie Holzer Schirm is a writer, community activist, photographer, sought-after speaker on the international stage, loving wife, mother, and grandmother. Before becoming an award-winning author of her debut nonfiction *Adventurers Against Their Will* and follow-on book, *My Dear Boy*, Joanie was in the business of engineering for thirty-five years, including sev-  enteen years owning and managing her own Orlando company. As the youngest daughter of Dr. Oswald "Valdik" and Ruth Alice (née Lequear) Holzer, she realized her unique family history had relevance for today. To inspire new generations not only to care but to care enough to act as peacemakers. Joanie's books appear in education programs and exhibits around the world.

Free lesson plans are available on her website www.joanieschirm.com and through organizations such as Arolsen Archives (formerly ITS), Florida Department of Education, National World War II Museum, and the Holocaust Memorial Resource & Education Center of Florida.

Contact Joanie Holzer Schirm at joanie@joanieschirm.com.

www.ingramcontent.com/pod-product-compliance
Lightning Source LLC
Chambersburg PA
CBHW071904290426
44110CB00013B/1270